VOLUME 12 • I.

MW00438950

GREAT COMMISSION
RESEARCH JOURNAL

Published by the Great Commission Research Network

© 2020 Great Commission Research Network

Published by the Great Commission Research Network (GCRN)
GCRN's Registered Agent: Corporation Service Company
7716 Old Canton Road, Suite C
Madison, MS 39110

www.greatcommissionresearch.com

Printed in the United States of America by Martel Press, Claremont, CA

Correspondence: 695 E. Bougainvillea St., Azusa, CA 91702 USA

All rights reserved. No part of this publication may be reproduced, stored in a retrieval system, or transmitted in any form or by any means—for example, electronic, photocopying, recording—without the prior written permission of the general editor of the journal. The only exception is brief quotations in printed reviews. Copyrights on articles are held by the Great Commission Research Network with permission to re-publish given to the authors. Requests for permission to reproduce material from the journal, except for brief quotations in scholarly reviews and publications, should be directed to the general editor at ddunaetz@apu.edu.

THE PURPOSE of the *Great Commission Research Journal* is to communicate recent thinking and research related to effective church growth and evangelism.

THE JOURNAL The *Great Commission Research Journal* (formerly, *The Journal of the American Society for Church Growth*) is published semi-annually, Fall and Spring. It is indexed in *Religious and Theological Abstracts*, *Christian Periodical Index*, and the *Index to Book Reviews in Religion, Religion Indexes: Ten Year Subset of CD-ROM*.

ISSN 1947-5837 (print)
ISSN 2638-9983 (online)
ISBN 978-0-9986175-7-2

THE OPINIONS AND CONCLUSIONS published in the Great Commission Research Journal are solely those of the individual authors and do not necessarily represent the position of the Great Commission Research Network.

GENERAL EDITOR:
David R. Dunaetz, ddunaetz@apu.edu
Azusa Pacific University, California, USA
ASSISTANT EDITOR:
Hannah Jung, hannahtrinity1@gmail.com
Azusa Pacific University, California, USA
BOOK REVIEW EDITOR:
Kelton Hinton, khinton247@gmail.com
Johnston Baptist Association, North Carolina, USA
EDITORIAL BOARD MEMBERS:
Moses Audi, mosesaudi@yahoo.com
Baptist Theological Seminary, Kaduna, Nigeria

PAST EDITORS: John Vaughan   1991-1995
                  Gary L. McIntosh   1996-2008
                  Alan McMahan   2009-2018
                  Mike Morris   2018-2020

CONTENTS

GREAT COMMISSION
RESEARCH JOURNAL
2020, Vol. 12(1) 1-17

CHURCH-BASED RESEARCH: CHALLENGES AND OPPORTUNITIES

David R. Dunaetz, Editor

Abstract

Because the church is the body of Christ, research focused on the Great Commission and Jesus' concern for evangelism and disciple-making needs to be church-based. The goal of such research is to better share God's love to a world who does not know him by building up a collection of knowledge that will enable us to do so. This research may be both theological (focusing on what the Bible and other theologians have said) and scientific (focusing on collecting new data and interpreting it, especially in light of theology). Church-based scientific research may be either qualitative (exploring broad ideas and phenomena in a relatively subjective way) or quantitative (testing specific ideas by collecting data measuring the variables of interest as objectively as possible). The Great Commission Research Journal *is an especially appropriate outlet for publishing such research.*

Church-Based Research: Challenges and Opportunities

The Church Growth movement (McGavern & Wagner, 1990; McIntosh, 2003; Rainer, 1998; Towns et al., 2004; Wagner, 1984; Warren, 1995), the Church Health movement (Schwarz, 1996), and the Missional Church movement (Guder, 1998; Tang & Cotherman, 2019;

Van Gelder & Zscheile, 2011) have produced a multitude of ideas concerning the nature of effective evangelism (Stetzer, 2006). There are dozens, if not hundreds, of principles that are said to be relevant to sharing the gospel with those who do not know Christ. Undoubtedly many, if not most, are true at least under some conditions. But how do we know which ones are true, and under what conditions? That is the purpose of research concerning the Great Commission: To discover the factors that influence the effectiveness of our efforts to obey the commandments that Jesus has given to us. This research must be church-based research because the local church is the body of Christ (I Cor. 12:27), the community of those who have been redeemed by their faith in Christ and the means by which God works through his people to accomplish his purposes.

What is Research?

Research is essentially what needs to be done to increase our knowledge about something. In some contexts, this can be as simple as reading what others have discovered about a topic. However, to gain new knowledge concerning a topic, that is, knowledge that does not currently exist, original research must be carried out which is based on what is already known about a topic and which uses methods that are likely to lead us to additional discoveries. In this sense, research is what results from science, "a set of methods used to collect information about phenomena in a particular area of interest and [to] build a reliable base of knowledge about them" (Bordens & Abbott, 2011, p. 2).

As Christians, we may feel a tension concerning research. Because we have God's Word and the Holy Spirit within us, we already have "all things that pertain to life and godliness" (2 Pet 1:3, ESV) and research may not seem necessary. Yet, when research is viewed as an effort to obtain new knowledge, the value of research becomes clearer, "The heart of him who has understanding seeks knowledge" (Prov 15:4, ESV), "An intelligent heart acquires knowledge" (Prov 18:15, ESV). Knowledge cannot replace the Bible or the work of the Holy Spirit in leading us to live a life pleasing to God, but the more knowledge we have of how people think, feel, and behave, the better we can respond in love to the needs of those around us (Phil 1:9). This means that church-based research, for the Christ follower, is not undertaken simply for the sake of gaining new knowledge; its overarching goal, rather, is to better love others by finding the most effective ways to respond to their needs, especially their fundamental spiritual needs, "For what does it profit a man to gain the whole world and forfeit his soul?" (Mark 8:36, ESV).

In this sense, church-based research or Great Commission (Mt. 28:19-20) research has as a subgoal to build up a collection of evidence, leading to knowledge, concerning conversion, disciple making, following Christ, baptism, teaching what Jesus instructed, and experiencing life together as Christ's body the church. Similarly, this research should provide explanations, rooted in evidence, of the phenomena we observe, such as numerical church growth (as well as stagnation or decline), spiritual growth of the individual, the Christian's use of skills and spiritual gifts in churches, and engagement in and commitment to the ministries of a church. To the degree we increase our knowledge concerning how and why these phenomena occur, we have successfully carried out Great Commission research.

Such research does not come naturally, even to Christian scholars who have been trained in the necessary methods. Such research requires both skepticism and intellectual humility (Swanson, 2005). Skepticism is needed because people, including (or perhaps especially) Christians, often make bold claims that may or may not be true. C. Peter Wagner, a founding member of the Great Commission Research Network, claimed, "The single most effective evangelistic methodology under heaven is planting new churches" (1990, p. 11). Is this true? Asking such a question requires a skepticism that might not be appreciated by those who have great respect and esteem for Wagner (among whom I count myself), or for those who live in a context where such a statement is considered a self-evident truth. Yet research may indicate that it is not always true, and that other forms of evangelism may be more effective in some contexts (cf. Bell & Davis, 2004). Such knowledge would be extremely useful but can only come from research rooted in a healthy level of skepticism.

Along with skepticism, high-quality research requires intellectual humility, an understanding that one's knowledge may be fallible and a willingness to change one's beliefs when presented with new evidence (Davis et al., 2016; Whitcomb et al., 2017). Few scientists believe that science can "prove" something (Popper, 1959; Stanovich, 2013);

rather, research provides evidence for a theory or model of a phenomenon that the researcher is trying to better understand. The data that we collect might be quite accurate, but our interpretation of the data may not be. For example, as humans, we often succumb to a *confirmation bias* (Nickerson, 1998), the tendency to interpret ambiguous information in a way that confirms our existing beliefs. To overcome this bias, we must humbly be aware of our own intellectual limitations, the limitations of our data, and our tendency to see what we want to see. Similarly, although we may believe Scripture to be inerrant or infallible, intellectual humility requires us to admit that our *interpretation* of Scripture may, at least occasionally, be errant or fallible.

Theological vs Scientific Research

Among Christians, there is a wide range of approaches to research. One way to classify them distinguishes between theological research and scientific research. Theological research, along with research in fields that emphasize history, applies systematic methods focusing on existing writings or documents along with logical reasoning to come to conclusions. These documents may include the Bible, historical documents produced by churches such as confessions and creeds, foundational writings by theologians (e.g., Calvin, Luther, and Wesley), or other theological treatises, essays, and research. Logical reasoning is then applied to come to conclusions relevant to the question or problem that is being addressed.

In theological research, generally no new data is collected nor are there empirical tests (e.g., repeatedly measuring a phenomenon in different conditions to understand how the conditions affect the phenomenon) to see if the conclusions are true. For example, in soteriology, the question of perseverance of the saints and/or synergism cannot be studied by putting people who self-identify as Christians into various situations and then observing which ones obtain eternal life. Rather, we discuss what the Bible says, what theologians have said, and the logical implications of the various concepts, perhaps seeking to integrate the material with contemporary concepts or to apply it to contemporary problems.

If God has truly revealed himself through Jesus Christ and the Scriptures, theological research lays the foundation for understanding not only our very existence, but also all that we can observe empirically. A theologically informed worldview enables us to understand the purpose of what we observe and enables us to view phenomena from an eternal perspective, rather than a simple temporal perspective. It enables us to understand observable phenomena from a macroscopic or "big picture" perspective, rather than a microscopic perspective that naturally results from a limited set of data.

Thus theological research depends heavily on the *method of authority* (Peirce, 1877) and *rationalism* (Descartes, 1637/2000). The method of authority, basing conclusions on what an accepted authority says on a topic, is only effective in discovering truth to the degree that the authority is correct. If the authority is the Bible and the Bible is the Word of God, then such an approach is quite justified, albeit potentially limited by our fallible interpretations mentioned previously. If the authorities are human theologians, the approach is likely to be less effective. Nevertheless, Calvin, Luther, or Wesley may be more reliable than @MiddleSchoolTheologian on Twitter. Another limitation of this method is that some fallible authorities are more vocal or available than others, contributing to the echo chamber effect (Colleoni et al., 2014) that is so visible on our Facebook feeds; we are likely to believe that the authorities which are the most accessible to us represent a consensus of all authorities we deem reliable, which may be far from the truth (Bordens & Abbott, 2011).

Similarly, rationalism (using reason to come to the knowledge of truth) in theological research has both strengths and weaknesses. Rationalism as a research method enables us to take the message of the Bible and make it relevant to today's context. This is one of the fundamental responsibilities of church leadership and the basis of all persuasive sermons. Its proper use is what makes most Christian books convincing. However, what is considered a clear and convincing argument for one person, may not at all be persuasive to another. Often, there are reasons to accept an argument in one direction as well as other reasons to accept an argument that goes in another direction. The number of unresolved theological debates in internet forums is a witness to the limitations of the rational approach to theology.

In contrast to theological research, scientific research, even church-based scientific research, does not seek to answer the big picture "Why?" and "For what purpose?" questions relevant to our existence. Rather, science is based on observation, interpreted by reason (Einstein, 1934). This empiricism, collecting and interpreting data based on real experiences, enables us to produce evidence useful for answering questions that revelation and rational thought alone may not be able to answer. Examples of such questions include "In what ways do twenty-first century North American Christians grow in their commitment to God in large churches compared to how they grow in their commitment to God in small churches?" and "Is pastoral narcissism tolerated in some cultures more than others?" Answers to such questions require observation and analysis and may significantly contribute to understanding how to better fulfill the Great Commission in our particular contexts.

At the center of the scientific method lies the idea of testing ideas. Our personal experience, what others claim to have experienced, or what we read in the Bible or elsewhere, accompanied by rational analysis, may lead us to tentative conclusions that may or may not correspond to objective reality, which, from a theological point of view, may be defined as God's perspective on the matter. If revelation or reason do not provide sufficient evidence, as is often the case given our penchant for being influenced by our self-serving biases (Forsyth, 2008; Miller & Ross, 1975), empirical data may provide additional evidence to evaluate such hypotheses. However, it should be noted that data can only provide support for hypotheses, not proof (Crano et al., 2015). Rival hypotheses or theories may also account for the data. However, consistent evidence producing support for our hypothesis makes the evidence stronger. On the other hand, a lack of support may indicate that our hypothesis or theory needs refining or that we collected the data in a way that did not capture the phenomena we wished to observe. With enough evidence, more complete theories will eventually eliminate rival theories because they better account for the evidence. For example, if evidence is consistently found that larger churches are more likely to attract narcissistic pastors than smaller churches (Dunaetz et al., 2018; Puls, 2020), pastoral search committees can adjust their strategies to find the most appropriate pastor to best serve God in their context.

Church-Based Scientific Research

For several decades, church researchers have sought to use scientific research to better understand how to fulfill the Great Commission. This desire to better understand the phenomena associated with disciple making lay at the heart of the Church Growth movement of the 1970s and 1980s and the origin of the *Great Commission Research Journal* (McQuilkin, 1974; Towns, 1986; Towns et al., 2004; Wagner, 1973). Scientific research focused on the Great Commission has also been adopted in other contexts such as the Evangelical Missiology Society (Rommen & Corwin, 1996), the Church Health movement (Schwarz, 1996), and, more recently, the Missional Church movement (Breen & Gustafson, 2019), contexts in which scholars have tried to avoid some of the extremes of the twentieth century Church Growth movement (Stetzer, 2012; Towns et al., 2004) but holding to the same general goal of effective evangelism and church development.

Several difficulties exist in conducting research focused on themes related to the Great Commission. Perhaps the most obvious is that the primary outcome variables with which we are concerned, for example, an individual's salvation, is only known to God, as described in the parable of the wheat and tares (Matt. 13:24-30). Humans can only look for outwards signs of salvation (James 2:24), whereas God looks at a person's heart (I Sam. 16:7). Nevertheless, there are many outward behaviors and internal attitudes in individuals which can be measured (e.g., the fruit of the Spirit and the works of the flesh, Gal. 5:19-23), and one's beliefs, such as the faith that is associated with salvation, can be at least approximately expressed by individuals (Rom. 10:8-10) and measured by researchers.

Other difficulties concern the fact that the discipleship to which Christ calls us is always within a community, the church which is in a very real sense the body of Christ (I Cor. 12:27). Most scientific research concerning Christians, such as those found in the *Journal of Religion and Health*, *Psychology of Religion and Spirituality*, and the *Journal for the Scientific Study of Religion*, focuses on phenomena which occur within individuals, such as outcomes concerning health and mental well-being, that is, clinical outcomes. Studies focusing on outcomes related to Christian communities or relationships between Christians are less common. Because discipleship takes place in the context of the body of Christ, that is, an organization comprised of individual Christians, church-based research shares some of the difficulties that are encountered in other forms of organizational research, namely, ethical limitations and accessibility issues (Spector, 2001).

Because research in organizations, including churches, always involves real people in situations that are part of their life, we can only rarely conduct research in laboratory contexts where interventions with no real-life consequences can be used to conduct an experiment. Most people, and especially Christ-followers, would consider it unethical to conduct an intervention in a church that could potentially have negative consequences, e.g., ask the pastor to give a series of fire-and-brimstone sermons one month and then to give a series of prosperity gospel sermons the following month, measuring the effect of each series on church members' behavior as the series progress. For this reason, surveys (rather than interventions) are more commonly used in church-based research. Rarely are there negative consequences to asking questions about one's beliefs, behavior, or health, especially when the surveys are anonymous. Similarly, unobtrusive observation can be used to collect data. However, this is limited to observable public behavior, such as counting the attendance in a worship service or observing how many people remain talking to people around them after the worship service ends for more than 30 seconds.

Another limitation of church-based research concerns accessibility. The unit of analysis, that is, the entity that is being analyzed in a study, may be either the individual, the small group, the church, or the network of churches such as the denomination. Collecting data from a sufficient number of entities can be very difficult. Suppose we determine that we need to collect data from 300 units to be reasonably sure of detecting a phenomena that we are interested in and of finding evidence strong enough that we can reasonably reject the idea that the results were obtained by chance (a typical desired sample size calculated by using a power analysis; Cohen, 1988). Finding 300 individuals to complete a survey may be doable. Collecting data on 300 small groups would be more difficult, as would be data on 300 churches. Collecting data on 300 networks would be more difficult still. This means that many studies that we would like to conduct will remain undone because collecting the data is beyond the means of most researchers. Nevertheless, Christ calls us to sacrificially love our neighbors (Mark 12:31, John 15:13), so we must be willing to pay the cost of discovering how to better love them whenever it is feasible.

The Church-Based Research Process

Figure 1 presents a simple model describing the church-based research process. These five steps (defining research objectives, research design, data collection, data analysis, and conclusions and reporting) provide a broad overview of how research can be done in churches and other contexts to understand how to better fulfill the Great Commission.

Figure 1. *The Church-Based Research Process (Dunaetz, 2020)*

Defining Research Objectives

The starting point for undertaking research is to clearly define one's research objectives. Does the researcher want to find out if an idea is true? Does the researcher want to better understand a phenomenon? Such questions may arise from the researcher's context, interests, or present needs. However, before defining the research objective, the researchers should become familiar with the previous research relevant to the topic (hence the arrow leading to the first step in the diagram). Researchers may start off by thinking they want to answer one question, but as they do a thorough review of previous research on the topic (commonly known as a literature review), they may realize that their question has already been answered, that there is a better or more important question to answer, or that the question needs to be reworked to maximize its usefulness or build upon previous research.

If the research is more general or exploratory in nature, a qualitative approach is often taken, that is, a rather subjective exploration of the subject to develop some ideas that might be true or generalizable to situations other than the exact situation studied (Creswell & Poth, 2016; Patton, 2014). Qualitative research is subjective in that it is difficult to separate the values and biases that researchers bring to the research from the conclusions that they make. For example, if one researcher believes that exegetical preaching is the most effective way to influence non-Christians, then he is likely to collect data (e.g., interviews with people) and will interpret it in a way that supports his existing beliefs. If another researcher believes that topical preaching is the most effective way to influence non-Christians, he also might collect data, perhaps even by interviewing the same people, but he is likely to interpret what they say as indicating that his existing beliefs about preaching are true.

Despite its subjectivity, qualitative research is still quite valuable. The studies described above would undoubtedly provide insight into the positive effects of both expository and topic preaching, especially in the context studied (Salkind, 2017). They also might provide information that is useful to choose between the two approaches in a different context. Such research might also contribute to the formulation of a theory of when expository preaching is most effective and when topic preaching is most effective, a theory that could be tested with the second broad category of research, quantitative research.

Quantitative research, in contrast to qualitative research, seeks to be as objective as possible, thus requiring an examination of much more narrow questions. Quantitative research seeks specifically to test the veracity of precise, limited statements, a process known as hypothesis testing (Fisher, 1925; Popper, 1959). Quantitative research is objective in that the researcher *operationalizes* the phenomena being studied by using clear definitions and procedures that can be used by other researchers. Thus quantitative research conducted by one researcher should lead to the same conclusion to which a different researcher would come, if they are using the same operationalizations and a sufficiently large and representative sample, and even if they start with different beliefs concerning the veracity of the hypothesis being tested or use different samples.

For example, in our preaching example, we may want to test the hypothesis that "Expository preaching has a greater influence on non-Christians than topical preaching" (or vice-versa). Both expository and topical preaching would need to be operationalized, perhaps with a questionnaire where auditors would indicate their agreement with a series of statements such as "The pastor spoke about a single passage in the Bible" (expository preaching) and "The pastor thoroughly addressed a topic that is relevant to today" (topical preaching). Such scales, typically consisting of a half-dozen to several dozen items, would need to undergo a series of validity and reliability tests to see if they are measuring what they are supposed to measure and if the measures are trustworthy. This is especially true because there is undoubtedly an overlap between expository and topical preaching and the two scales would be correlated to some degree. If the scales are trustworthy, they would be able to be used by other researchers to measure the degree to which an expository or topical message was heard by the auditor. Similarly, the influence that a sermon has on the non-Christian listening to it would need to be operationalized, perhaps by asking them a series of questions on how persuasive they found the sermon to be or to what degree they intend to change something in their life because of the sermon. Once the variables in questions are operationalized, a research design is chosen to test the hypothesis in a relatively objective way that should not depend on the presuppositions of the researcher.

Research Design

Once the research question or hypothesis is well defined, the researcher needs to develop a plan for obtaining the relevant data. In theological research, this is often an extended literature review, perhaps seeking to apply texts, documents, or past research to the research question in a new way or a new context.

In qualitative research, the research question may be answered in a number of ways (Creswell & Poth, 2016), perhaps via a case study or a biographical (narrative) study. More complex approaches include phenomenological research (describing how people have experienced a phenomenon), grounded theory (developing a theory based on people's experience), or an ethnography (a description and interpretation of a group's culture). Jay Moon's (2020) article in this issue is an example of grounded theory, a study resulting in a theory of choosing a form of alternative financing for a church, based on its assets and relational networks. The researcher must determine the most appropriate method of qualitative research based on their research questions, available resources, and their abilities. Data is typically collected through interviews, but may also include observations, focus groups, surveys, or artifacts, such as existing documents, artwork, or audiovisual materials.

In quantitative research, the principle research designs are either experimental or correlational. Experimental research designs, with random assignment of participants to one or more conditions, are preferred because they can demonstrate causation. If two groups are composed of individuals randomly assigned to different conditions (e.g., a service where the pastor preaches topical sermons and a service where the pastor preaches exegetical sermons), then any difference in group outcomes greater than what would be expected by chance is most likely due to the difference in conditions. However, such studies are difficult to carry out well in churches. Besides the ethical issues discussed previously, all confounding variables must also be controlled (e.g., time of service, relationships of people attending the service, the pastor's preference of styles, and a myriad of other potential confounds).

For these reasons, most quantitative research designs in churches are not experiments but are correlational in nature, seeking to understand if two or more variables are related to each other or if there is a difference between specific groups of people. Such correlational studies can use easy-to-complete surveys with multiple-choice items, making them much more feasible. Nevertheless, great care must be used to operationalize the variables measured in order to have credible results. The correlations calculated can only describe how different phenomena move with each other; they cannot demonstrate that a change in one variable is caused by a change in another variable. Evidence for causation must be argued indirectly when an experimental design is not possible.

Data Collection

Once the researchers have prepared the interview protocol, the survey, or any other tool to be used to obtain the information needed, they may move toward data collection. Before data is collected, often the research protocol must be reviewed and approved by the Institutional Review Boards of the organizations with which the researchers are affiliated and by the appropriate authorities in the church or churches being studied.

Data for qualitative research most often comes from interviews. The researchers may have a fixed interview protocol used for all the participants, or the interviews may be less structured where the interviewer may adapt the questions according to the responses of the person being interviewed and to what has been learned in previous interviews. The researchers should continue to interview people until they reach *saturation*, the point where they sense that they are no longer getting new information relevant to the research question from additional interviews (Saunders et al., 2018).

Data for quantitative research in churches most often comes from surveys that measure all the variables in the hypotheses along with demographic information about the participants. The scales used to measure each of the variables should be psychometrically valid, so it is advisable to use preexisting scales for the variables in question, scales that have already proved their worth. Anonymity should be assured to maximize the likelihood of honest answers. The number of surveys needed (typically about 300) should be calculated with a power analysis before data collection begins. This prevents "fishing expeditions" and "*p*-hacking" where the researcher collects data until something interesting shows up, a process which makes the results less trustworthy (Head et al., 2015).

Data Analysis

After the data is collected, it must be analyzed. In qualitative research, this can be done manually, or with the help of software (Creswell & Poth, 2016). The quality of the analysis, which is necessarily subjective, is heavily dependent on the skills of the researcher. The goal is to make sense of the data collected and to synthesize it in a way that provides at least partial answers to the research questions. The researchers must make a strong case that the data means what they claim it means.

In quantitative research, statistical analyses are performed on the data, in the manner determined at the time when the research was designed. Researchers often team up with statistical consultants for this analysis (and for the research design) as statistics are notoriously tricky and not easily mastered by the non-specialist. The goal is to determine if the data supports the hypothesis or not. If it appears highly unlikely that the results did not occur by chance (i.e., there is less than a 5% chance of getting these results if the hypothesis were not true), we say that the results are significant and that we have found evidence to support the hypothesis. If the results are not significant (i.e., there is more than a 5% chance of getting these results if the hypothesis were not true), we cannot make any conclusions; the hypothesis may be true, but it may not be. Finding support for the hypothesis is generally considered strong evidence since the research is designed to be as objective as possible, but there is always up to a 5% chance that the results were spurious, due to chance, not resulting from an actual phenomenon that could be expected to occur in other situations.

Conclusions and Reporting

After the data is analyzed, the researchers determine what they can conclude and create a report, providing details of how the study was conducted, the results, and an argument for their conclusions. For church-related studies, especially those related to evangelism and disciple making, submitting the resulting article to the *Great Commission*

Research Journal is an excellent choice for disseminating the research to scholars and practitioners who have a heart for ministry. Before being accepted for publication, the article will be peer-reviewed, typically by at least two specialists. Based on the reviewers' comments, there will be a recommendation to either "reject," "revise and resubmit," "accept with conditions," or "accept unconditionally." If the recommendation is either of the middle two, the researcher is invited to rework the paper in light of the reviewers' comments and recommendations. The result is almost always a stronger paper.

The process for conducting research, including church-based research, is often slow and frustrating. Receiving a critical review of one's work can be painful and maddening, but after a week or so, the researchers often find that the reviewers' criticisms seem more reasonable. The goal of the *Great Commission Research Journal* is to publish high quality, trustworthy peer-reviewed research that is useful for others as they work to love and serve others through the proclamation of the gospel. As the editor of the *Great Commission Research Journal*, I encourage you to clarify the question you want to answer, design the research so as to find what you need to know, collect and analyze the data, and to write up the results so that a multitude of others may be able to benefit from your discoveries and the gospel may more effectively be proclaimed throughout the world.

David R. Dunaetz, General Editor

References

Bell, S., & Davis, R. (2004). Church planting as growth strategy: Is it effective? *Ministry, 76*(4), 18-26.

Bordens, K. S., & Abbott, B. B. (2011). *Research design and methods: A process approach* (8th ed.). Mc Graw-Hill.

Breen, M., & Gustafson, D. (Eds.). (2019). *Missional disciple-making: Disciple-making for the purpose of mission.* 3dm International.

Cohen, J. (1988). *Statistical power analysis for the behavioral sciences* (2nd ed.). Lawrence Erlbaum Associates.

Colleoni, E., Rozza, A., & Arvidsson, A. (2014). Echo chamber or public sphere? Predicting political orientation and measuring political homophily in Twitter using big data. *Journal of Communication, 64*(2), 317-332.

Crano, W. D., Brewer, M. B., & Lac, A. (2015). *Principles and methods of social research* (3rd ed.). Routledge.

Creswell, J. W., & Poth, C. N. (2016). *Qualitative inquiry and research design: Choosing among five approaches.* Sage

Davis, D. E., Rice, K., McElroy, S., DeBlaere, C., Choe, E., Van Tongeren, D. R., & Hook, J. N. (2016). Distinguishing intellectual humility and general humility. *The Journal of Positive Psychology, 11*(3), 215-224.

Descartes, R. (1637/2000). *Discourse on method and related writings*. Penguin.

Dunaetz, D. R. (2020). *Research methods and survey applications* (3rd ed.). Martel Press.

Dunaetz, D. R., Jung, H. L., & Lambert, S. S. (2018). Do larger churches tolerate pastoral narcissism more than smaller churches? *Great Commission Research Journal, 10*(1), 69-89.

Einstein, A. (1934). On the method of theoretical physics. *Philosophy of Science, 1*(2), 163-169.

Fisher, R. A. (1925). *Statistical methods for research workers*. Oliver and Boyd.

Forsyth, D. R. (2008). Self-serving bias. In W. A. Darity (Ed.), *International encyclopedia of the social sciences* (2nd ed., Vol. 7). Macmillan Reference.

Guder, D. L. (Ed.). (1998). *Missional church: A vision for the sending of the church in north America*. William B. Eerdmans Publishing.

Head, M. L., Holman, L., Lanfear, R., Kahn, A. T., & Jennions, M. D. (2015). The extent and consequences of p-hacking in science. *PLoS Biology, 13*(3), e1002106.

McGavern, D. A., & Wagner, C. P. (1990). *Understanding Church Growth* (Third ed.). Eerdmans.

McIntosh, G. L. (2003). *Biblical church growth: How you can work with God to build a faithful church*. Baker Books.

McQuilkin, J. R. (1974). *Measuring the Church Growth movement*. Moody Press.

Miller, D. T., & Ross, M. (1975). Self-serving biases in the attribution of causality: Fact or fiction. *Psychological Bulletin, 82*(2), 213-225.

Moon, W. J. (2020). Alternative financial models for churches and church plants: When tithes and offerings are not enough. *Great Commission Research Journal, 12*(1), 19-42.

Nickerson, R. S. (1998). Confirmation bias: A ubiquitous phenomenon in many guises. *Review of General Psychology, 2*(2), 175-220.

Patton, M. Q. (2014). *Qualitative research & evaluation methods: Integrating theory and practice* (4th, Ed.). Sage Publications.

Peirce, C. S. (1877). The fixation of belief. *Popular Science Monthly, 12*, 1-15.

Popper, K. (1959). *The logic of scientific discovery*. Routledge.

Puls, D. (2020). *Let us prey*. Cascade Books.

Rainer, T. S. (1998). *The book of Church Growth*. B&H Publishing Group.

Rommen, E., & Corwin, G. (Eds.). (1996). *Missiology and the social sciences: Contributions, cautions, and conclusions*. Evangelical Missiological Society Series. William Carey Library.

Salkind, N. J. (2017). *Exploring research* (9th ed.). Pearson.

Saunders, B., Sim, J., Kingstone, T., Baker, S., Waterfield, J., Bartlam, B., Burroughs, H., & Jinks, C. (2018). Saturation in qualitative research: Exploring its conceptualization and operationalization. *Quality & Quantity, 52*(4), 1893-1907.

Schwarz, C. A. (1996). *Natural church development: A guide to eight essential qualities of healthy churches*. Churchsmart Resources.

Spector, P. E. (2001). Research methods in industrial and organizational psychology: Data collection and data analysis with special consideration to international issues. In N. Anderson, D. S. Ones, H. K. Sinangil, & C. Viswesvaran (Eds.), *Handbook of industrial, work and organizational psychology* (Vol. 1, pp. 10-26). Sage.

Stanovich, K. E. (2013). *How to think straight about psychology.* Pearson.

Stetzer, E. (2006). The evolution of church growth, church health, and the missional church: An overview of the church growth movement from, and back to, its missional roots. *Journal of the American Society for Church Growth, 17*(1), 87-112.

Stetzer, E. (2012). What's the deal with the Church Growth movement? Part 2: Some unfortunate evolutions. *The Exchange with Ed Stetzer.* https://www.christianitytoday.com/edstetzer/2012/october/whats-deal-w-church-growth-movement-part-2-some.html

Swanson, R. A. (2005). The challenge of research in organizations. In R. A. Swanson & E. F. Holton (Eds.), *Research in organizations: Foundations and methods of inquiry* (pp. 11-26).

Tang, L., & Cotherman, C. E. (Eds.). (2019). *Sent to flourish: A guide to planting and multiplying churches.* IVP Academic.

Towns, E. L. (1986). The relationship of church growth and systematic theology. *Journal of the Evangelical Theological Society, 29*(1), 63-70.

Towns, E. L., Van Gelder, C., Van Engen, C., Van Rheenen, G., & Snyder, H. (2004). *Evaluating the Church Growth movement: 5 views* (P. E. Engle & G. McIntosh, Eds.). Zondervan.

Van Gelder, C., & Zscheile, D. J. (2011). *The missional church in perspective: Mapping trends and shaping the conversation.* Baker Academic.

Wagner, C. P. (1973). 'Church Growth': More than a man, a magazine, a school, a book. *Christianity Today, 18*(5), 11-14.

Wagner, C. P. (1984). *Leading your church to growth.* Regal Books.

Wagner, C. P. (1990). *Church planting for a greater harvest: A comprehensive guide.* Regal Books.

Warren, R. (1995). *The purpose driven church : Growth without compromising your message & mission.* Zondervan.

Whitcomb, D., Battaly, H., Baehr, J., & Howard-Snyder, D. (2017). Intellectual humility: Owning our limitations. *Personality and Social Psychology Bulletin, 43*(6), 793-813.

GREAT COMMISSION
RESEARCH JOURNAL
2020, Vol. 12(1) 19-42

ALTERNATIVE FINANCIAL MODELS FOR CHURCHES AND CHURCH PLANTS: WHEN TITHES AND OFFERINGS ARE NOT ENOUGH

W. Jay Moon

Asbury Theological Seminary, Wilmore, Kentucky, USA

Abstract

Many churches face financial strains, forcing some to close every year. Similarly, potential church plants may be delayed or disbanded due to a lack of finances. Instead of relying solely on tithes and offerings, this article provides six non-traditional financial approaches that churches can implement to promote financial viability and missional impact. The interaction of the church's financial liquidity (low or high) and relational networks (closed or open) provides a starting point to determine which approach may be best in the church's context. Practical applications are provided through examples of contemporary churches using these approaches.

What can a church's leaders do when tithes and offerings are simply not enough to meet the church budget? For example, Highland Heights Baptist Church[1] of Memphis, Tennessee, dwindled in size from its glory days of several hundred people to only 25 active members, resulting in the plummeting of tithes and offerings. If major expenditures arose such as a leaky roof or water boiler failure, then the church would not have known where to turn since their income would not be able to cover these expenses. Three nearby aging churches had already closed due to similar problems. The remaining few people scattered throughout the large worship space were silently asking themselves, "When will we need to close our doors?"

A church planting team had a similar problem. They were passionate about their vision but after several months of difficult fundraising, the team leader asked himself, "Will we ever raise the money that we need to get this church started?" Common church planting financial models recommend the planting team to raise money upfront for the first three years' budget before the launch, perhaps $300,000 to $500,000 for a typical church plant in the U.S.[2] How many teams can raise this amount of money? Even more importantly, how many more churches could be planted if this requirement were eliminated?

Such examples are all too common in the North American church context. This year alone, about 4,000 churches will likely close. There are various reasons for the closures, but financial concerns are often an important factor. About 4,000 churches are likely to be planted this year as well.[3] Many will not survive long due to financial considerations. Is it possible that we are relying upon outdated church financial models that are not always viable in the 21st century? Perhaps non-traditional financial options for churches and church plants need to be explored.

What if tithes and offerings are not enough to meet the church budget? How do leaders inject new life into older churches and plant more churches in light of such financial challenges? This article explores six non-traditional financial approaches for churches that can enable them both to meet their budget and to fulfill their mission. Instead of a "one size fits all" approach, context-specific factors will influence which of the options will be the most suitable. Examples will demonstrate that these approaches are not simply the product of wishful thinking; rather, existing churches and church plants are already utilizing these approaches, resulting in both financial viability and missional impact.

Background

Mark DeYmaz and Harry Li (2019), in their book *The Coming Revolution in Church Economics*, predict that the financial models of many American churches will not be sustainable in the future. The Boomer and Builder generations are responsible for most of the church giving presently. As they age, the generations following them are not only attending church less often, but they are more prone to tipping instead of tithing. This is reflected in less giving as a percentage of income to American churches (even while giving to charitable causes overall has risen slightly).[4] While churches have benefited from property tax exemption and clergy housing credits, there has been talk in recent years of these benefits being rescinded, particularly as governments are looking for ways to support the social services desired by voters.[5] DeYmaz and Li conclude that tithes and offerings will no longer be sufficient to financially support many churches in the 21st century because of the reductions in church attendance, giving, and tax exemptions.[6] How will pastors and church planters, who are called by God, find sufficient finances to support themselves and their churches?[7]

MINCE Approaches

The acronym "MINCE" lists five non-traditional approaches that churches may use to weather the financial storms. Leaders should not mince words when talking about finances; instead, leaders should be clear and straight to the point concerning the following five approaches:

1. **M**onetize existing church resources
2. **I**ncubate new businesses
3. **N**on-profits form mission arms of the church
4. **C**o-vocational pastoring opens multiple income streams
5. **E**ntrepreneurial churches locate church inside the marketplace

Each of these approaches can more effectively utilize the assets already available to the church. Much like the foolish servant in the parable of the talents, many churches have buried their underutilized talents. Profit earned in a godly manner is not ungodly; rather, the Lord is pleased when five talents are turned into ten and angered when the one talent is buried (Matthew 25:14-30). What could happen if churches unbury their assets and consider other financial approaches?

In short, non-traditional approaches may greatly reduce the number of church closures and increase the number of church plants. Experience over the last five years with churches that are using these non-traditional financial approaches in the U.S. and abroad demonstrates that these methods work This is not simply wishful thinking. Like any movement, there are innovators whose early experiences provide wisdom and insight that can benefit others. Some pastors and church planters are already implementing these approaches and their experiences will enable others to avoid the dangers described by DeYmaz and Li (2019).[8]

A Church's Context

Leaders in every church need to consider their context to determine the best approach. Figure 1 describes how two variables, financial liquidity and relational networks, interact to create contexts propitious to the various approaches.

Financial Liquidity

From a business standpoint (Mueller, 2019), financial liquidity "refers to how easily assets can be converted into cash. Assets like stocks and bonds are very liquid since they can be converted to cash within days. However, large assets such as property, plant, and equipment are not as easily converted to cash" (par. 1). A church may have a range of assets available, such as buildings or land with low financial liquidity and cash which has the highest financial liquidity. Owning primarily low financial liquidity assets often leads a church to a scarcity mentality and low-risk taking. On the other hand, owning primarily high financial liquidity assets leads to an abundance mentality and entrepreneurial thinking due to the ready availability of cash. In Figure 1, the horizontal axis represents the financial liquidity of the church's assets, from frozen (low financial liquidity) to fluid (high financial liquidity).

Relational Networks

When researching how people came to faith, Win and Charles Arn (1988) found the vast majority (from 75% to 90%, depending on the context) came to church due to an invitation from a friend or family member.[9] These relational networks are crucial for church planters. Donald McGavran (1981) considered these relational networks of family and friends so important to church growth and health that he labeled them "bridges of God." Church growth specialist, George Hunter (2009, p. 66) concludes that "churches grow as they reach out across the social networks of their people, especially their newest converts." When these relational networks are *open*, church members have easy access to and frequent discussions with those outside the church. Relational networks, however, can be *closed*, which occurs when Christians no longer maintain or develop relationships with people outside the church. This can be due to several factors such as moving, interpersonal conflicts, and neglect. One common reason that networks close is that new Christians often stop socializing with their old friends.[10] A church's relational network can range from closed to open. At one end of the continuum, some churches are closed, primarily consisting of members who do not have relational networks of people whom they can invite to church. On the other end of the continuum, some churches are open, having many members with relational networks of people with whom they regularly and freely engage outside the church, in their neighborhood, at work, on social media, or elsewhere. In Figure 1, the vertical axis represents the church's relational networks, from closed to open.

Interaction of Financial Liquidity and Relational Networks

Significant insights concerning church sustainability come from examining the intersection of these two factors. These insights may indicate which of the MINCE approaches are most suitable. However, these five approaches are not mutually exclusive; churches may find it wise to use a combination of approaches. Figure 1 is simply meant to provide a starting point to help a church flourish once again.

Figure 1: *Financial Approaches Available to Churches as a Function of Relational Networks and Financial Liquidity*

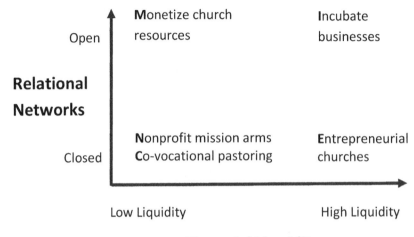

Monetize[11] Existing Church Resources

Some churches have very little access to cash (low financial liquidity), yet their relational networks are strong and open (the top left position in Figure 1). This means members still have access to people outside the church who interact with them and trust them. Highland Heights Baptist Church was in this position. As their attendance dwindled, so did their cash reserves. This is an opportune time for the church to recognize and then monetize their existing resources. For example, many churches heat and cool a building that is left empty most of the week. This creates a resource that can be monetized, which can provide an income stream as well as meet needs in the community.

Wilmore United Methodist Church in Wilmore, Kentucky, recognized their building was greatly underutilized. Moreover, local millennials in the gig economy were looking for workspaces to avoid boredom and to connect with others for personal and professional reasons. Such needs have led to the creation of coworking spaces across the country where young entrepreneurs rent a desk, sometimes with access to copiers, meeting rooms, coffee, restrooms, and important relational connections. Mazareanu (2019) notes, "Coworking is a new but fast-growing trend in the United States - from only 14 spaces in 2007, the number of coworking and other shared, collaborative office spaces increased to 4,043 in 2017." Several coworking companies have arisen to fill this need.[12] What could happen if churches filled this need and offered coworking space for rent? When Wilmore UMC was approached by some millennials with this need, 23 people (primarily seminary students) signed up. This not only provided an income stream for the church, but it also addressed a specific need of these millennials who now recognize the church as relevant to the concerns and issues that they face.

Other churches are also opening their buildings for coworking space during the week, such as Real Life Church in Richmond, Virginia. Pastor Svetlana Papazov (2019) calls this a "church for Monday" since its missional purpose is to "close the perilous Sunday to Monday gap by uniting worship on Sunday to work on Monday" (p. 24). Pastor Papazov, however, has taken this a step further by providing, not only coworking space, but business and life coaching in the Real Life Center for Entrepreneurial and Leadership Excellence.

From a missional perspective, the popularity of Airbnb among millennials who are looking for an experience as they travel[13] challenges Christians to do what they should do: be hospitable. Airbnb provides an incentive for Christians to practice hospitality by opening rooms for rent. At the same time, Airbnb offers the opportunity to connect with others for discussions about faith. Churches can open a parsonage or other space to travelers who are thankful for the accommodation. Again, this not only provides an income stream for the church but also enables the church to meet the needs of the community via hospitality. The result can be fresh missional engagement. Using Airbnb to find paying guests to welcome into my house has led to many faith-focused discussions as well as some guests even coming to church with me.

These financial approaches are open to churches with limited cash since they usually require few funds to operate. Entrepreneurial church members may seize this opportunity and provide money upfront to re-arrange or repair space so it can be monetized in this way.[14]

What approach would be useful if these churches and church plants with open relational networks already had more cash available?

Incubate New Businesses

When cash is more available (financial liquidity is high) and the church has open relational networks, then it is in a position to consider incubating new businesses (Figure 1, top right). This requires upfront financing, but it may produce a cash flow in a relatively short time. When a church has cash available, this approach can often provide a better return on investment than simply parking the money in a bank. The liquid assets provide the finances necessary for such an undertaking, while the open network provides a customer base for the new business.

For example, Shadowland Community Church in Nicholasville, Kentucky, purchased a coffee shop in the center of the city. The goal was to provide a third space for the community during the week as well as to provide a church venue on Sunday.[15] This space has also provided a venue to incubate several other businesses. The coffee shop business provides a rental income stream to the church.[16] One of the church members has opened a counseling center in the same building, which also provides rent to the church. On Sunday, this room is used for childcare. The church also rents out the upstairs as an event space throughout the week. This event space served over fifty different groups in its first year. Some of these groups pay rent (wedding rehearsal dinners, birthday parties, photo shoots) while others were not charged. Once again, this provides not only a financial stream but also helps the church to interact with the community missionally. For example, Shadowland Community Church has opened the space for receptions after the funerals of high school students as well as for students to study during their final exams, providing free pancakes for them as they study. On Sundays, the event space is used for Sunday School.

Shadowland Community Church is not unique, however. A church in Kansas City, Missouri, rents out their building as a wedding space for $3,000 a night. The pastor informed me that the building is booked most Friday and Saturday nights throughout the year. The church also provides space for an event planner and a photographer to incubate their businesses inside the church building. The equipment is put away and the rooms are then used for Sunday School by the church on Sundays.[17]

Some churches are even more creative with the use of their space to incubate businesses. DeYmaz and Li's church in Little Rock, Arkansas, rented a part of their building to a group that created a gym which is now heavily used during the week. Since this facility generates income that is not directly related to the mission of the church, the workout business pays the tax liability based on the percentage of the building that they use.[18] This business provides a significant portion of the church's income.[19]

This approach is not simply for business-friendly neighborhoods. Bible Center Church in the Homewood neighborhood of Pittsburgh, Pennsylvania, is in a neighborhood that has long been plagued by poverty and crime. Pastor John Wallace's passion for black-owned businesses has resulted in the church incubating a variety of businesses through their Oasis Project. This initiative has spawned a transportation company, a café, a farm, a fishery, a business development center, a property maintenance and management company, and an entrepreneurship academy. Several entrepreneurs recently helped include a jewelry maker, a chef, a web designer, and an event planner. Pastor Wallace (2019) explained that this approach is driven by a missional vision, "I believe that the proliferation of small [business], even microbusiness, ownership can have a tremendously powerful impact, not only economically, but also psychologically, on communities like Homewood." Ultimately, this strengthens the financial position of both the community and the church.

Jeff Greer and Chuck Proudfit (2013) in Cincinnati, Ohio, are taking similar steps by establishing what they call biznistry, meaning a "faith-based business that generates profits for ministry" at Grace Chapel (p. 18). The Grace Chapel campus, a former manufacturing plant, provides new business incubation, acceleration, funding, training, and team building in order to launch biznistries. There are now over two-dozen biznistries connected to the Grace Chapel campus which have created over 100 jobs, bringing thousands of people to Grace Chapel's campus each week. They are also earning about $200,000 in profits annually for ministry reinvestment (20% of the annual operating costs of the church).[20] The motivation for each of these biznistries is "to create purpose-filled, meaningful work in the business world that advances the kingdom of God" (Greer and Proudfit, 2013, p. 52).

While biznistries attempt to use people's market skills and networks to change lives and reveal the kingdom of God, others are using non-profit organizations to do the same.

Non-Profit Organizations Form Mission Arms of the Church

Many churches have limited cash and their relational networks are shrinking or closed (the bottom left of Figure 1). While this combination appears bleak, there is potential for these churches to become missionally vibrant and financially viable again.

Could a church increase its mission budget to over half a million dollars without asking for more tithes and offerings? This is what Mosaic church in Little Rock, Arkansas, accomplished through the formation of a non-profit arm called "Vine and Village." Since this non-profit is separate from the church, Vine and Village attracts government grants and donations from other entities that would not give to the church. Even other churches are donating to this non-profit due to its missional impact. A separate nonprofit organization becomes a mission[21] arm of the church when it contributes to the well-being of the community by assisting immigration, training teen moms, offering fresh produce to 'food deserts,' providing an extended family to those with disabilities, offering a chess club, opening a clothes closet, or providing employment training or any other service that meets needs in the community.[22]

Joy Skjegstad has worked with over 50 churches to assist in the formation of non-profits. She currently directs the Park Avenue Foundation, which is a nonprofit connected to Park Avenue United Methodist Church in South Minneapolis. Skjegstad (2002) notes that "Setting up a nonprofit at your church can bring together the very best aspects of the church with the outside resources that a nonprofit can draw" (p. 3). She further explains how churches have several advantages for starting non-profits compared to individuals:

1. Churches often have the trust of the community so that the church can draw participants that may not otherwise feel safe at other locations.
2. Churches have a built-in and skilled volunteer pool that may enable the non-profit to function well. The talent within a church can provide substantial services to the community. Skegstad (2002) explains from her own experience at Park Avenue, "Volunteer tutors, mentors, lawyers, doctors, and nurses were all mobilized from within the congregation to do good works every day of the week in the church building" (p. 3).
3. Since a church itself is considered a non-profit entity by the Internal Revenue Service, members of the church often possess the needed expertise to furnish the necessary structure and paperwork for a nonprofit.

Some churches have operated schools and daycare centers as nonprofit entities. The nonprofit can pay fair market rent (or less) to the church. This allows the church to once again receive an income stream as well as missionally impact the community through the social services provided by the non-profit. A pastor in a small community in Kentucky recently informed me his church would have closed a long time ago if it were not for the preschool in the church providing both an income stream and new relationships. Once again, both missional impact and financial viability can be achieved through this approach.

Co-vocational Pastoring Opens Multiple Income Streams

Another approach for churches that have both low financial liquidity and closed or shrinking social networks (the bottom left of Figure 1) is to consider co-vocational pastoring. Previously, the term bi-vocational was used to describe a pastor who worked another job outside the church. The implication was that this was a temporary situation until the church could afford a full-time salary. Once the church could afford it, the pastor would leave his or her secular job and work full-time for the church. In contrast, the term 'co-vocational' assumes that the pastor will continue to work outside the church even when the church can afford a full-time salary.[23] In this way, the church can be more generous to serve the community as well as create relational networks through the pastor's employment (Briscoe, 2018).

Shadowland Community Church is a co-vocational church. Five teaching pastors share the preaching but only one is paid part-time for mission mobilization. The church has a goal to give away 51% of the tithes and offerings to impact the community to reveal the kingdom of God. This is unheard of for most churches since the personnel and building costs typically absorb a large majority of the budget.

After discussing alternate church financial models with a bishop for the Church of God in Christ (COGIC), he revealed that this co-vocational approach is used by almost all of the churches in the denomination. This is due to financial reasons as well as missional purposes. This was not a new practice; instead, he assumed this was (and would continue to be) the normal practice for COGIC pastors.

Pastor Johnson Asare in Ghana, West Africa, said, "In the garden of Eden, God provided multiple streams. Perhaps, this is to ensure that there was water even if one stream dried up. Pastors also need more than one income stream because you never know which one will dry up."[24] Pastor Asare is a co-vocational pastor who has started businesses such as a hotel, a shea butter processing station, and a cashew farm. He states that he does not need money from outside of Ghana to do church planting and ministry. Located in a Muslim majority city, the money for Christian ministry comes from Muslims who patronize his businesses.

Karl Vaters (2017), in *Christianity Today*, calls bi-vocational ministry the "new normal" since it has increased 32% from 2010 to 2015.[25] There is a growing number of pastors who are adopting this approach for both financial and missional reasons. Since the marketplace is a relational network where people exchange products and services of value, the co-vocational approach may open relational networks as well as provide additional income.

What if the marketplace was not simply a venue for the pastors' job and ministry, but was a mission venue for the entire church?

Entrepreneurial Churches Locate Church Inside the Marketplace

If the church has high financial liquidity and closed relational networks (the bottom right of Figure 1), then the financial model identified as entrepreneurial churches should be considered. Entrepreneurial churches are defined as

> communities of Christ followers among unchurched people through businesses in the marketplace. Entrepreneurial Church Plants address the need to engage public society through the marketplace via entrepreneurial means. Such entrepreneurial church planters either start new businesses or work within existing businesses to plant churches in business venues (Moon & Long, 2018, p. 6).

Paul Unsworth in London, England noticed that 20,000 people a day walked down his street each weekend, yet there was no vital Christian witness in the neighborhood.[26] Only 5% of the British attend church regularly (Brierly Consultancy, 2015). How could he gain access to this large group of people and lead them to Jesus? His response was to open the Kahaila coffee shop that serves high-quality coffee and cake. Unsworth explains his rationale,

> We need to find out how to form community. This is why we chose a coffee shop. It is a third space where people share life. We aim to build community in the café.
>
> For evangelism, if you like doing something, do it with others. Invite others to do it with you. You build community and listen to others.[27]

This has resulted in a church plant that also meets in the building on Wednesday nights. He is motivated by a missional impulse to connect with the unchurched and is finding success. Unsworth shared,

> I have had more spiritual conversations with people in a week than I had in working in a church for a whole year... people that don't know anything about Jesus. We need to create opportunities to genuinely listen to people. In time, they will be interested in what I believe. Church is more than a service on a Sunday. Church is a spiritual family that comes together to redeem the lost.[28]

Unsworth is not unique in this approach (Moon & Long, 2018). Instead of starting a new business, Sean Mikschl works as a waiter in an existing business (Copper River restaurant). This provides an open network for his church plant that meets on Thursdays at 11 PM, the time when restaurant workers end work, and are ready to meet.

Several venues have been used successfully to start entrepreneurial church plants such as workout facilities, bakeries, barbershops, hotels, and cafes, in addition to numerous coffee shops. There are even networks to encourage the opening of 'micro-churches' in the marketplace.[29] This approach can open up relational networks when financial liquidity is high but current relational networks are closed.

Decentralized Churches

After hearing about the above five financial options recently, a pastor said to me, "In my situation, I do not know where to start since I am not even on your chart! My cash is so limited and my networks are so minimal that I do not even fit into any of these options. What can I do?"

Fortunately, there is another option for church planters and struggling churches. This can be described as Decentralized Churches. Hence the sixth option (starting with the letter D) updates the MINCE acronym to MINCED. Decentralized churches are sometimes known as house churches, simple churches, organic churches, dinner churches, fellowship bands, or micro-churches.[30] What they all have in common is the gathering of small groups of Christ followers in everyday settings. The venues vary, as well as the number of people and the meeting frequency. They challenge the existing financial models because they do not assume that the Sunday church attendance is the most accurate measure of church health or that bigger is always better. As a result, this eliminates (or greatly reduces) the largest line items for most church budgets: mortgages, rent, and salaries.

Similar to the other MINCE financial options, this model can be both missional and financially viable. For example, the Inspire Movement in both Europe and the U.S. focuses on missional engagement and discipleship as a starting point for gathering a community of Christ followers. The Tampa Underground network includes house churches that focus on mission among the poor, the homeless, those in recovery, single mothers, and many more.[31]

The recent COVID-19 pandemic has revealed a strength of decentralized churches. When large church gatherings were suddenly prohibited, many churches struggled to adopt technology such as Zoom to maintain their connections with their congregations. Hugh Halter explains how decentralized churches hardly skipped a beat amidst the pandemic,

> Are all churches struggling? No, in fact, if we understand and believe the reports that half the American church has already been decentralized into house churches then only half the church is struggling. "Where is the missional movement?" so many have asked the last five years? Well, the real answer is that the missional church, with decentralized form, is alive and well. Like cockroaches to the coronavirus, we know how to navigate and even prosper among the rubble. We already know how to live off the meager scraps. We are everywhere and we're healthier now than ever before.[32]

One of the surprises of the Coronavirus has been that churches have been forced to decentralize to survive. This reminds us of biblical and historic times when the church survived and even thrived amidst great struggle and persecution. A bigger surprise is that some churches are now asking the question if they want to return to the centralized 'church as normal' once the social isolation bans are lifted.

As with all of the MINCED options, some risks need to be considered before aiming to adopt one of these financial models.

Cautions to Consider for MINCED

Discussions of money in churches may be a sensitive topic. On the one hand, theologians like John Wesley recognized the great potential for wealth to be created and used to transform society. David Wright (2012, p.95) notes, "Wesley's publishing enterprise was enormously successful. It made Wesley very wealthy. Some estimate he earned as much as 30,000 pounds (more than $6 million today) over his life from this highly successful entrepreneurial business." Reflecting on the missional significance of business and money in the marketplace, Wesley concluded, "It is therefore of the highest concern that all who fear God know how to employ this valuable talent [money]; that they be instructed how it may answer these glorious ends, and in the highest degree."[33]

On the other hand, Wesley recognized the dangers of riches. While money can be used for great good, it can also be used for selfish gain and harm. As a result, there are some precautions to consider as pastors and church planters seek economic wisdom.[34]

Single Versus Triple Bottom Line

Instead of relying upon a single bottom line for business (i.e., profit), Wesley warned employers not to harm workers physically or mentally through their work. He also warned against work that was profitable but not beneficial for society. Today, we would identify these as social considerations. Those making business decisions must consider social and spiritual consequences (in addition to the financial consequence which determine how long a business will last) in order to mitigate against the excesses of the free market system. In short, just because a business deal can be done profitably does not mean that it should be done. If there are negative social and spiritual consequences, even though there are positive financial consequences, then it is not a good deal.[35]

Accountability

Wesley was adamant that Christians should be in accountability groups. For entrepreneurs, these groups should ask questions like, "How much money did you make this month?" and "What did you do with it?" Wesley encouraged entrepreneurship but not for selfish accumulation. His dictum, "Make all you can, save all you can, and give all you can" is best understood by looking at the final goal: to help the poor. Accountability in business and spirituality is one way to guard against selfish excess.

Generosity

Wesley felt that money should not find a resting place in one's soul. Money is called currency, hinting that it should move and not become stagnant. He felt that it was not a sin to be wealthy, but it would be sinful to die wealthy. Wesley's own use of money serves as an example. "He kept none of this money [$6 million] for himself. All but the barest of necessities was reinvested in the work of the movement" (Wright,

2012, p. 95). In this way, generosity is a guard against greed and stockpiling wealth.

Taxes

If churches operate businesses that are not crucial to the mission of the church, then the IRS requires the church to pay Unrelated Business Income Tax, even though the church is a non-profit entity. The best way to pay this tax is to require the business or businesses operating on church property to pay it.[36]

Commodification

In a market society, there is a temptation to put a value on everything, which can reduce people to simply customers or commodities, thereby damaging relationships. This can be particularly harmful in a church where relationships are meant to be more familial than market-based. For example, I encourage pastors to be wary of pyramid schemes in their churches since they can do much damage if members develop relationships with motives other than love. Making decisions based on the triple bottom line mentioned above can reduce the pull toward commodification.

Jesus Overturning the Money Changers' Tables (Matt. 21:12-13)

Some claim that these passages warn against mixing business and church. Rather, this is a rebuke of greedy business practices, particularly practices that rob the poor, as well as a lack of prayer in church. The approaches described above attempt to return prayer to the marketplace as well as promote business that is done with integrity and honesty. DeYmaz and Li (2019) recommend that the church consider itself a 'benevolent owner' and that the businesses operated inside the church are charged a fair and even below-market rent for the use of the church space. Profit should not be viewed negatively. Jesus commends the faithful steward who makes five talents from the five talents that were given to him. How many of today's churches are simply sitting upon their talents instead of engaging the marketplace to create more? They may mistakenly use these passages on the cleansing of the temple to justify their inaction.

Teamwork

Several of the above approaches highlight the need for teamwork. Since pastors seldom make good bankers (Greer & Smith, 2016), it is best to team with others who are skilled in accounting, finance, marketing, and strategic planning. There are typically people in the church who are skilled in these areas since that is what they do professionally. They often develop enthusiasm for a ministry when they hear that their skills are needed and can be put to use for the kingdom.

Charging for Blessings

In Acts 8, Simon the sorcerer tried to purchase spiritual blessing from Simon Peter and John. The harsh rebuke by the apostles should remind us that spiritual blessings are gifts from God for which we should not charge people.

Conclusion

Former Anglican Bishop Graham Cray has noted, "The long-established ways of doing church are working less and less."[37] He could very easily have been referring to the changing financial picture of the church as well as its missional effectiveness. The financial challenges facing churches call for new approaches to meet their budgets beyond simply the collection of tithes and offerings.

While there is no quick fix to the financial difficulties facing churches and church plants, considering the interaction of a church's relational network (closed or open) and financial liquidity (low or high) provides useful options for both financial viability and missional vibrancy. This argument is not meant to demean tithes and offerings. On the contrary, they are essential for the church and its members. On the other hand, this article has attempted to address the question, "How does the church survive if tithes and offerings are not enough to meet the church's budget to fulfill its mission?"

Consider again Highland Baptist Church in Memphis, Tennessee. Instead of demolishing their 76-year-old building, they recognized that they could monetize their greatest resource, the building. Presently, the Collegiate School of Memphis operates a middle school and high school in the building during the week while the church continues its services on Sunday. The nondenominational Avenue Community Church also meets in the building. These three organizations support Heights CDC, a nonprofit community development corporation working to improve the economy, housing, green spaces, and community identity in the neighborhood. What has been the result?

Larry Reed with the Collegiate School of Memphis has observed that new life has been breathed into the church and community, "In 2006 or 2007, if you would have driven by those buildings, they were either vacant or largely unused by the church and minimally, if at all, maintained. Now they have lots of life."[38] In addition to financial stability, Christina Crutchfield (Heights CDC community engagement coordinator) explained how the church and school are also having a missional impact in the community, "Collegiate is a great partner with the neighborhood because instead of just existing ... they actually go out into the neighborhood and do service projects."[39]

What can church leaders do when tithes and offerings are not enough? They can consider the MINCED financial options. This may make the difference between shuttering operations or bringing life back into the church.

Notes

[1] To learn more about this church's journey, see
https://www.highgroundnews.com/features/SavingChurchesHeights.aspx
[2] I heard this figure from a presentation made by a representative of Stadia (one of the largest church planting networks in the U.S.) at the Exponential church planting conference in Orlando, FL, in March 2018. The figure may be even more now.
[3] Accurate numbers for church plants and closings are not easy to obtain. These estimates are from a 2019 conversation with Dr. Winfield Bevins, Director of Church Planting at Asbury Theological Seminary.
[4] https://pushpay.com/blog/church-giving-statistics/
[5] The potential rescinding of the church property tax exemption was prominent in national news again in November, 2019 when a presidential candidate said, "Yes" when asked if he thought "religious institutions like colleges, churches, and charities, should lose their tax-exempt status if they oppose same-sex marriage?" (Lybrand, H. and Subramaniam, T., 2019).
[6] I whole heartedly affirm the collection of tithes and offerings. This article, though, offers creative approaches to use the resources at the church's disposal to reveal

the kingdom of God when tithes and offerings are not sufficient to meet the budget for various reasons.

[7] The COVID-19 situation has further aggravated this situation. In May 2020, CapinCrouse noted that 56% of all churches experienced a decline in overall giving. Of the churches that experienced a decline, 41% noted that this decrease was 2-10%. See the report: https://www.capincrouse.com/wp-content/uploads/2020/04/CapinCrouse-2020-Impact-of-COVID-19-on-Church-Giving.pdf

[8] For an updated discussion on church economics amidst the Coronavirus, see the webinar led by Mark DeYmaz: https://www.youtube.com/watch?v=hj3QC8aovXE

[9] Win and Charles Arn (1988) interviewed 17,000 people and asked, "What or who was responsible for your coming to Christ and to your church?" Following Arn's research, Gary McIntosh (2014) did a similar survey in 2000 with 1,000 participants and found some changes whereby the friend and family influence reduced to 58.9%, and 17.3% came to Jesus and church through a church staff member. Even still, the family and friend connection was by far the leading influence.

[10] Hunter (2009, p. 62) considered the relational networks of new believers to be particularly crucial for church growth for the following reasons: "(a) New disciples still have many more contacts with pre-Christian people than long-established members have. (b) They still remember what it was like to try to make sense of one's life without Jesus Christ as Lord; many longtime members have forgotten. (c) Their faces and lives still reflect the contagion of a new discovery; many friends and relatives knew them "BC." (d) They have not yet had time to become linguistically corrupted by theologians and preachers; they still understand and speak the language of the secular marketplace. So, for such reasons, growing churches often have a very intentional, deliberate, ongoing practice of reaching out to people in the networks of their newest members and Christians."

[11] Monetize is the "process of turning a non-revenue-generating item into cash." See: https://www.investopedia.com/terms/m/monetize.asp

[12] WeWork has capitalized on this need for work spaces and relational connections across the U.S. (Bliss, 2018).

[13] As of November, 2019, Airbnb states that they have experienced a 153% compound growth rate since 2009 with 150 million total users worldwide and over half a billion Airbnb stays all-time. Millennials account for roughly 60% of all guests who have ever booked on Airbnb. $20,619 is the average expected annual profit of Airbnb hosts renting out a full two-bedroom apartment or house in major cities. For these and further statistics, see Bustamante, J. (2019).

[14] I know entrepreneurs who are willing to enter into rental arbitrage with these types of facilities. This means that the entrepreneur will pay the church a set monthly amount for rent, then they will use the Airbnb or work collective market to increase their income above the amount of the rent.

[15] Actually, two churches now meet in this same space on Sunday (when the business is closed). In addition to SCC meeting on Sunday morning, a church that ministers to the recovery community meets on Sunday night.

[16] At the time of this writing, the owner of the coffee shop closed her business, but another entrepreneur is preparing to open a bakery/dessert service there. This demonstrates the flexibility and continuance of businesses in a particular space.

[17] In this case, the church monetizes their underutilized asset by charging rent (the first approach) while the church or community members incubate a business (second approach). The end result puts the church and community in a stronger financial position.

[18] This is called Unrelated Business Income Tax or UBIT. Churches should ask the business entity to pay this tax based on the % of the building that they are using. In this way, the church protects their non-profit status while still complying with IRS tax rules.

[19] DeYmaz and Li (2019) recommend that churches find entrepreneurs in the church to start small businesses based on the existing services that the church provides. For example, instead of the church giving away free (and poor quality) coffee, they could create a coffee business that sells coffee and uses some of the profits for ministries in the church (e.g., youth group expenses). In this way, the small business benefits the church and community financially and missionally.

[20] According to an email from Chuck Proudfit to the author on 12/12/19.

[21] Vine and Village started from the holistic work of the church, as they attempted to integrate three components for community transformation, as described by their mission statement, "To be a catalyst to serve people living in and around Little Rock's emerging University District by helping to meet their social, economic and spiritual needs resulting in *Real Community Transformation*." See: https://vineandvillage.org/about-us-3/

[22] Started in 2008, this non-profit seeks to transform the community through spiritual, social, and economic means. Under the leadership of its executive director, Paul Kroger, this ministry continues to expand. See: https://vineandvillage.org/

[23] SEND Institute commissioned a survey of bi-vocational pastors in 2018 and found that "41% indicated that being bi-vocational was integral to a long-term ministry strategy," indicating that they were co-vocational (Yang, 2019).

[24] Based on a personal conversation with Johnson Asare in 2014.

[25] Based on a 2015 Faith Communities Today survey, fewer than two-thirds (62.2 percent) of U.S. churches have a full-time pastor. That's down from 71.4 percent in 2010. That means that bi-vocational pastoring went from 28.6% in 2010 to 37.8% in 2015. For African American pastors, the bi-vocational rate soars to 57% (Vaters, 2017). For further trends in bi-vocational ministry, see Earls, A. (2016).

[26] Based on a conversation with Paul at the Kahaila coffee shop in 2019.

[27] https://www.youtube.com/watch?v=ma-RQfrBmqk

[28] https://www.youtube.com/watch?v=eLEEh1K_W8g

[29] For example, there are over 200 micro-churches in the Tampa Underground. For more information, see: https://www.tampaunderground.com/our-microchurches. In addition, Common Thread in Birmingham, Alabama, has incubated over 14 businesses. For more information, see: https://commonthread.org/

[30] One could also place the multi-site option in this list, but the multi-site option has a more central hub than the others listed. I know of several financially challenged churches that have reached out to a larger church in order to become

one of their sites. This has kept the struggling church open while also allowing more lay involvement.

[31] https://www.tampaunderground.com/our-microchurches

[32] https://outreachmagazine.com/interviews/54120-cockroaches-and-the-coronavirus.html

[33] Sermon by John Wesley, "The Use of Money." Wesley's sermons are available at: Wesley Center Online (n.d.). Several of his sermons dealt with topics related to money, including:

- o   Sermon 87 - The Danger Of Riches   1 Tim 6:9
- o   Sermon 112 - The Rich Man And Lazarus   Luke 16:31
- o   Sermon 50 - The Use Of Money   Luke 16:9
- o   Sermon 51 - The Good Steward   Luke 21:2
- o   Sermon 108 - On Riches   Matt 19:24
- o   Sermon 126 - On The Danger Of Increasing Riches   Ps 62:10

[34] While there is not enough space in this article to discuss the theological underpinnings of economic wisdom, see the Economic Wisdom Project (n.d.) for helpful resources.

[35] For a further discussion on the balancing of financial, social, and spiritual capital, see Danielson (2015).

[36] For a helpful resource on UBIT, see: Batts, Michael E. (2020). *Unrelated Business Income and the Church: The Concise and Complete Guide – 2020 Edition.* Orlando, FL: Accountability Press.

[37] Personal conversation with the author and Graham Cray in York, England in January 2017.

[38]https://www.highgroundnews.com/features/SavingChurchesHeights.aspx

[39] Ibid.

References

Arn, W., & Arn, C. (1988). *The Master's Plan for Making Disciples: Every Christian an Effective Witness Through an Enabling Church* (2nd ed.). Baker Books.

Batts, M. E. (2020). *Unrelated Business Income and the Church: The Concise and Complete Guide - 2020 Edition.* Accountability Press.

Bliss, L. (2018, February 5). How WeWork Has Perfectly Captured the Millennial Id. *The Atlantic.* https://getpocket.com/explore/item/how-wework-has-perfectly-captured-the-millennial-id?utm_source=pocket-newtab

Bradley, J. D. *Church Giving Statistics, 2019 Edition.* Pushpay. July 18, 2018. https://pushpay.com/blog/church-giving-statistics/

Brierley Consultancy (2019, December 6). Christianity in the UK: Measuring the Christian population in the UK. *Faith Survey.* https://faithsurvey.co.uk/uk-christianity.html

Briscoe, B. (2018). *Covocational Church Planting: Aligning Your Marketplace Calling and the Mission of God.* Send.

Bustamante, J. (2019, November). Airbnb Statistics. *Property Management.* https://ipropertymanagement.com/airbnb-statistics

Danielson, R. (Ed.). (2015). *Social Entrepreneur: The Business of Changing the World.* Seedbed Publishing.

DeYmaz, M., & Li, H. (2019). *The Coming Revolution in Church Economics: Why Tithes and Offerings are No Longer Enough and What You Can Do About it.* Baker.

Earls, A. (2016, September 29). Second Shift: Thriving in Bivocational Ministry. *Lifeway.* https://factsandtrends.net/2016/09/29/second-shift-thriving-in-bivocational-ministry/

Economic Wisdom Project (n.d.). *Oikonomia Network.* https://oikonomianetwork.org/economic-wisdom-project/

Greer, J., & Proudfit, C. (2013). *Biznistry: Transforming Lives Through Enterprise.* P5 Publications.

Greer, P., & Smith, P. (2016). *Created to Flourish: How Employment-Based Solutions Help Eradicate Poverty.* Hope.

Halter, H. (2020, April 7). Cockroaches and the Coronavirus. *Outreach.* https://outreachmagazine.com/interviews/54120-cockroaches-and-the-coronavirus.html

Hunter, G. G. (2009). *The Apostolic Congregation: Church Growth Reconceived for a New Generation.* Abingdon Press.

Lybrand, H., & Subramaniam, T. (2019, October 11). Fact check: O'Rourke said he would support removing tax-exemptions for religious institutions that oppose same-sex marriage. Is that legal? *CNN politics.* https://www.cnn.com/2019/10/11/politics/beto-orourke-lgbtq-gay-marriage-church-fact-check/index.html

Mazareanu, E. (2019). Number of coworking spaces in the United States from 2007 to 2022. *Statista.* https://www.statista.com/statistics/797546/number-of-coworking-spaces-us/

McGavran, D. (1981). *The Bridges of God* (2nd ed.). Fuller Seminary Press.

McIntosh, G. (2014, October 29). What Person Led You to Faith in Christ? *Good Book Blog, Talbot School of Theology.* https://www.biola.edu/blogs/good-book-blog/2014/what-person-led-you-to-faith-in-christ

Mueller, J. (2019, July 14). Financial Liquidity. *Investopedia.* https://www.investopedia.com/articles/basics/07/liquidity.asp

Moon, W. J., & Long, F. (Eds.). (2018). *Entrepreneurial Church Planting: Engaging Business and Mission for Marketplace Transformation.* GlossaHouse.

Papazov, Svetlana. (2019). *Church for Monday: Equipping Believers for Mission at Work.* Living Parables.

Skjegstad, Joy. (2002). *Starting a Nonprofit at Your Church.* Alban Institute Series. Rowman & Littlefield.

Tatum, L. (January 15, 2020). Faith in Action: Sharing space to save historic churches, *High Ground.* https://www.highgroundnews.com/features/SavingChurchesHeights.aspx

Vaters, K. (2017, December 12). The New Normal: 9 Realities and Trends in Bivocational Ministry, *Christianity Today.* https://www.christianitytoday.com/karl-vaters/2017/december/new-normal-9-realities-trends-bivocational-ministry.html?paging=off

Wallace, J. cited by Gannon, J. (2019, November 4). Bringing Business Back to a Blighted Neighborhood, *Pittsburgh Post-Gazette.* https://www.post-gazette.com/business/bop/2019/11/04/Homewood-entrepreneurship-business-pittsburgh-Bible-Center-Church/stories/201910210110

Wesley Center Online (n.d.). http://wesley.nnu.edu/john-wesley/the-sermons-of-john-wesley-1872-edition/the-sermons-of-john-wesley-theological-topic/.

Wright, D. (2012). *How God Makes the World A Better Place: A Wesleyan Primer on Faith, Work, and Economic Transformation.* Christian's Library Press.

Yang, D. (2019, February 5). Convergence of Vocation: A Covocational Primer for Church Planting Networks. *Send Institute.*
https://www.sendinstitute.org/covocational-primer/

About the Author

W. Jay Moon, PhD, served 13 years as a missionary with SIM, largely in Ghana, West Africa. He is presently a Professor of Evangelism & Church Planting and Director of the Office of Faith, Work, and Economics at Asbury Theological Seminary. He has authored four books, including *Intercultural Discipleship: Learning from Global Approaches to Spiritual Formation* in the Encountering Mission Series by Baker Academic. He can be contacted at: jay.moon@asburyseminary.edu

GREAT COMMISSION
RESEARCH JOURNAL
2020, Vol. 12(1) 43-53

THE POWER OF FAITHFULNESS IN RELATIONAL EVANGELISM

Lance C. Hahn

Bridgeway Christian Church, Roseville, California, USA

Abstract

Many evangelistic efforts bear little fruit. It may be due to our inability to convey the right information, but it may also be due to an inappropriate environment for the information to be interpreted correctly. This article describes a process that God may use to engage a person whose heart has been prepared, so that the seed sown is received, not only as truth, but with joy. Relational evangelism carried out faithfully allows consistent sowing until chaotic moments open the heart.

God is a God of order.

When the earth was formless and void God illuminated the universe and fashioned the earth into a beautiful and orderly habitation. When winds raged and waves crashed, Jesus calmed them with a word. When the young demon-possessed slave girl heckled Paul the Apostle for days on end, he cast out the spirit and peace descended upon her.

God has always mended broken things and turned messes into redemptive epics. Therefore, where darkness and confusion reign, the

Kingdom of God shines the brightest. This is most true in the lives of people. God's most cherished creation draws his attention like none other. His love knows few bounds when it comes to protection, rescue, and salvation.

Humans, on the other hand, respond to chaos with desperation, ill-equipped to deal with uncertainty and disorder. When the façade of control is broken open, mankind faces its impotence, its fragility, its lack. It is then that a person is willing to have a dialogue about the things that matter, about the One that matters.

The Case for Relational Evangelism

The best and healthiest form of evangelism is done through meaningful and heartfelt relationships. Although 'cold call' methods were effective in the past, that day is most likely gone. With access to technology that allows detailed filtering systems, and due to decades of bitterness from advertising bombardment, it is almost impossible to start a meaningful conversation with a stranger. In the church I pastor, Bridgeway Christian Church, the single most common reason that people have come to our church over the last twenty-two years is word of mouth. Back in 2003, when we were a small church, I drew a family tree of how our congregation was connected, placing the name of every family in a bubble and attaching it to the person or means through which, or through whom, they came to Bridgeway. Almost every bubble was tied to another family or person with whom they had a significant relationship. In 2018, I again examined the origins of our congregation by holding a live poll on the weekend of December 15th through the 16th. Over 2000 congregants engaged in the electronic survey and the results were similar to the previous results.[1] Most people, 78.4%, when asked how they first heard of Bridgeway, responded "from a family member or a friend." Similarly, 90.3% responded "through a family member or friend" to the question, "How did you first learn about Christianity?" After two decades of ministry at this church, it has become clear that most people come to faith in Jesus Christ through a close and trusted relationship.

Nevertheless, as a North American Church, we have desperately tried alternative methods to reduce the time needed and to avoid the intimacy demanded for relational evangelism. We have attracted a few through impressive programs, but time, attention, love, and relationships are always more effective. Today is no different from yesterday. People in the post-modern world are craving connections. They are refusing to respond to modern mass ministry. But since we, as ministers are busier than ever, we try again and again and again to shorten the process and mass-market it. It is not working.

Ed Stetzer says, "Postmoderns do not fit into a nice little cultural box, but all people with a postmodern mindset have this in common: They need to be reached with the gospel of Jesus Christ, and the current pattern of church isn't reaching them."[2] The attractional model of "Let's make it better and maybe then they'll come" is a misnomer. Dan Kimball, in his book, *They Like Jesus But Not the Church: Insights from Emerging Generations*, wrote in 2007, "People who need to hear the gospel most likely aren't going to their church. On Sundays, they are sleeping in, shopping at the flea market, going out to breakfast – they're anywhere but at a church meeting. I don't know why we think that if we have good preaching or add a worship band or have coffee and candles that they will come. Those things are all good, but people outside the church aren't looking for a church with those things. They aren't looking for a church at all."[3]

I am as guilty as anyone. I dream of a world where people hear about what great things are happening in my church and come through the door by the droves. I want them to crave the messages I have prepared, experience the hospitality my team has created, soak up the environment we have crafted, and eagerly scoop up the visitor's mug on the way out, looking forward to next week's service. And yet, ironically, I do not want those same people wandering into a Mormon church or a Buddhist temple merely out of curiosity and find something attractive there. I would hope that they have a trusted friend with whom they can talk to help them know what they would be walking into. That is exactly what is happening when people visit churches. Someone walking into Bridgeway Christian Church for the first time is most likely with a friend or family member with whom they have a relationship. All the programs and warmth only matter to them once they are in the door, brought by someone with whom they have a relationship.

In their book, *The Master's Plan for Making Disciples,* Win and Charles

Arn say, "The conclusion is clear: The majority of people today can trace their 'spiritual roots' directly to a friend or relative."[4] It is for this reason that we need to focus on the already existing relationships that church members have with people outside the church. Dr. Gary McIntosh, in *Growing God's Church: How People Are Actually Coming to Faith Today,* explains, "There is a direct connection between the number of unchurched friends the adult worshipers of your church have and the potential growth of your church."[5] But how do we achieve this potential growth? All of us have friends and family who need to receive Christ but whom we have not brought to church. All of us have had conversations about the Lord that have not been productive. Michael Parrott reports in *Street Level Evangelism: Where is the Space for the Local Evangelism?* that "99 percent of the leadership ministries believe that every Christian, including leadership, has been commanded to preach the gospel to a lost world…[yet] Ninety-five percent of all Christians have never won a soul to Christ."[6] Even Pastors and church leaders do not seem to be personally bringing people to the Lord. Among my friends who are pastors of churches in Northern California, very few, if any, actively evangelize their friends and family personally. If we, pastors and church leaders, struggle to evangelize those whom we love, how can we expect our congregants to reach the world around them?

There are hundreds of great evangelism and church growth books. I am the last one who should be giving professional advice since I am not blessed with the gift nor calling to the office of evangelist. But I am a follower of Jesus and for that reason, I am called to do the work of an evangelist, whether it comes naturally to me or not. So, what can I offer to the plethora of opinions about the how, the why, the when, and the where of sharing our faith effectively? I can only propose my personal experience and what I have seen work in my own context.

The Chaos Effect: The Open Door

Pastor, author, and discipleship expert Mike Breen of the ministry 3DM, speaks of the "Person of Peace,"[7] mentioned by Jesus in chapter 10 of both the Gospel of Matthew and of the Gospel of Luke. Specifically, Luke 10:5-6 (NEV) says, "Whatever house you enter, first say, 'Peace be to this house!' And if a son of peace is there, your peace will rest upon him. But if not, it will return to you." Some ministry opportunities bring a person face to face with someone open to the gospel and some do not. Christ's instruction was that his followers should spend more time focusing on those 'people of peace' rather than with people behind a door that remains closed.

This concept of receptivity is what I call the *Open Door*. Although we are biblically called to cast a wide net across cultural boundaries, forcing us out of our comfort zone, it is clear that some people have been prepared by the Holy Spirit to receive the gospel and some have not. The Lord tells us, "No one can come to me unless the Father who sent me draws him."[8] This means that no matter how hard we try, no matter how smooth and winsome our methods, no matter how many evangelism books we have read, we will never get through to someone whom God has not prepared. It is rarely possible to discern who has and who has not been prepared from a distance. Usually, we only know whether people are prepared after we interact with them, up close and personal. Until we know with certainty that someone is called or not, it is wisest to continue loving and dialoging with them in case there is a barrier they need to get past in order to open up.

Not only does it depend on the person, but it can also depend on the *time* and *situation*. It is my opinion that God is constantly whispering to everyone on the planet and that there are certain times when God speaks more loudly. Periodically, the communication becomes more intense to get the person's attention. Will we be there for our friends when God opens up their hearts?

God has many ways to open someone's heart. Sometimes it is his kindness that leads to repentance.[9] But often it is hardship. The hardship may come in the form of struggle, fear, confusion, godly sorrow, or a host of other tribulations. Bad dreams and circumstances introduced King Nebuchadnezzar to Daniel and Joseph to Pharaoh. Leprosy connected Naaman and Elisha. Sorrows and loss drove men and women to the feet of Jesus during his earthly ministry. The same is true today. I wish it were not that way and I suppose God feels the same. Jesus taught that those who have hardship are blessed, for they will finally be open to God. The struggle creates the open door.

Difficulty tests existing constructs. For the most part, human beings rely on ideas and concepts that are tenuous at best. They organize their lives around a false sense of safety and have confidently built a house of cards. When those cards fall down, when chaos enters into their seemingly orderly lives, they recognize what is missing. George G. Hunter writes, "People become more receptive to involvement with a church during a season of their lives when they are 'between gods.' They have given up on whatever they most recently relied upon to complete their lives and are open to something else."[10] Everyone goes through difficult times. Every person on the planet gets slapped in the face with reality once or twice. At those times people are more open to the idea that all is not under their control and that they need help from someone greater than themselves.

So, we must look for an opportunity to present the Truth to whom the Lord has prepared. Such an opportunity occurs when a person's heart is softened, when the soil is tilled and receptive. We never know when that will be, so we need to be consistent, faithful lovers of people, steady servants, and ever ready beacons of hope. We are to be friends at all times, but we are most helpful when our friends go through difficult times. If we have not been a safe and wise friend to them during the bright times, they will not seek us nor trust us in the dark times. This requires steady faithfulness.

Examination of Motives

The motives for sharing our faith are important. I have been in ministry long enough to know that motives for ministry are varied and they are not always altruistic. When ministering to people in their point of pain, we need to examine our motives. If our motives are self-serving, the process will go wrong, and the person will likely end up worse than before. To take advantage of someone in their time of need is deplorable. Ends do not justify the means. Although someone may pray a prayer of salvation under coercion, that does not mean that it is sincere. The amount of baggage that can accumulate during an inappropriate evangelistic effort is staggering.

There is only one good motivation for evangelism, love. The early church did it for the right reasons. Michael Green, in *Evangelism in the Early Church,* says,

"This gratitude, devotion, dedication to the Lord who had rescued them and given them a new life, this sense of being commissioned by him and empowered by his Spirit to do the work of heralds, messengers and ambassadors, was the main motive in evangelism in the early Church. These people had been gripped by the love of God which had taken concrete form in the person of Jesus…Magnetized by this love, their lives could not but show it, their lips could not help telling it."[11]

George Hunter III, in his book *The Church's Main Purpose*, says, concerning coercion, "The early disciples did not seem to try to 'sell' people on following Jesus for any other 'benefits'. His benefits, like healing and exorcism, were apparently extended to people in need whether they ever became disciples or not; some did, some did not."[12] Many times Christians see only the statistics and not the hearts behind the statistics. It is vital that we love people whether they go to the altar or not. The world does not need more religious people taking advantage of desperate situations to peddle their goods. Followers of Christ need to respond to the opportunities that God provides and to love others steadily in order to make a difference when the doors open.

Appropriate Ministry at the Critical Moment

If we saturate our relationships and friendships with love, if we purify our motives, if we cautiously follow the Holy Spirit into that sensitive opening of doors, if we are faithful in the good and bad times and finally an opportunity comes, what do we say? What do we do? Too many times we freeze up when someone finally opens up to us. We may fear saying the wrong thing or fail to have answers. Surprisingly, most of the ministry has already been done before that critical moment. What we have done previously speaks louder than the words coming out of our mouth at that moment. Therefore, we must be faithful in our love and purposeful in our relationship building. When the chaos hits our loved ones, the Holy Spirit has assured us that he will give us the words to say because this moment is more important to him than it is to us. What does this look like?

When someone's life is turned upside down by pain, loss, grief, sorrow, fear, anxiety, or depression, our concern for them compels us to ease the pain and find a solution for them. Although we cannot personally solve their problems, we know the One who can. It is in the darkest hour of their lives that Jesus makes the most sense. It is when the shiny lights and the shimmering glitter are gone that the deep questions of life surface: Who am I? What am I doing here? What truly matters? Those are questions that lead to life-changing conversations. Those moments are opportunities to do what our love begs us to do for our friends, present the hope and help found in the gospel. We are not taking advantage of a situation, we are utilizing what we have been given to bring healing to those whom we care about the most, in their most challenging time.

We must listen more than we talk. When we finally speak it needs to be with love and tenderness. This is not the time for blame, it is a time for solutions and Jesus is their solution. He may not fix all of their surface problems and he may not remove their pain and loss, but he will certainly begin a process of restoration. The Bible tells us that, although bad things happen to good people, Jesus' love for his followers brings transformation. Jesus is a master at redemption. He takes bad situations and makes them better, glorious. He can feel people's pain and hold their hand in the darkness. He is not afraid of what we are afraid of. Our job in those moments is to communicate the truth to our friends and loved ones. The truth that Jesus loves them and cares for them. The truth that this world is broken, and that we all need a Savior. The truth that it will not always feel like this because the Comforter, the Holy Spirit, knows how to pick up all the pieces of a broken heart and put them back together. It is not our role to make unrealistic or inappropriate promises to make them feel better. We do not have to. We have access to the "Good News." The gospel is not a set of facts that they need to memorize while they contemplate their depravity, the gospel is the truth about the possibility of a relationship with their Creator. Whatever they are going through right now, it will be far better to walk hand in hand with one who is omniscient, omnipresent, and omnipotent. What they need is an introduction to him.

Let me share a personal example. As a high school senior, I was involved in a rock band. A young sophomore kid, who played guitar and had long hair like me, took a liking to me and we played music on and off together. We struck up a friendship. He did not have a church background, nor was he one to talk about feelings. I was loud about my faith but received little confirmation that he was listening or cared. Then one day after a girl broke his heart, he called me. He revealed to me that he too wanted to be a Christian like I was since it seemed to make such a big difference for me. To me, it was out of the blue. To the Lord, it was right on time.

Here is another more recent example from our small group ministry leader. She wrote to me, "I've been messaging a young woman who was interested in joining our Missional Community. She's new to town, doesn't have family or community here, and has experienced a lot of loss and pain over the last few years. Social anxiety and distance from God have also compounded her pain and isolation." This young leader explained that after a series of no-shows and after many invites, she felt led to invite her one more time. To the leader's surprise, the young woman came and had a wonderful time and joined the community. The pain in her life in that season was so great that God broke down her fear, isolation, and hardness of heart so that she might receive him. She is now a part of our congregation. If the small group leader had not been so faithful in inviting her even when it looked fruitless, this story would have turned out very differently. But she was a faithful friend and the Lord took advantage of it.

What About the Rest of the Time?

What do we do while we are waiting for the "open door" brought about by the chaos of life? What fills the days when our neighbor's life is not in shambles and everything seems to be going wonderfully? Is there a ministry mandate during the good times when people are feeling self-sufficient with no need for a Savior? Yes, there is. Although we turn up our intensity during times of opportunity, we are still to live as Christians. That means we are to love faithfully regardless of the visible outcome. It means that while we are developing relationships with the people around us, we are sowing seeds. We may pay special attention to people dealing with chaos in their life, but we do not ignore other people. We are not spiritual ambulance chasers.

When Donald McGavran wrote the book, *Understanding Church Growth*, he addressed this concept of receptivity and the concern that may arise when we adjust our ministry efforts to respond to open hearts. He wrote,

> "Recognition of variations in receptivity is resisted by some mission thinkers because they fear that, if they accept it, they will be forced to abandon resistant fields. Abandonment is not called for. Fields must be sown. Stony fields must be plowed before they are sown. No one should conclude that if receptivity is low, the Church should withdraw mission. Correct policy is to occupy fields of low receptivity lightly. They will turn receptive someday. They also have children of God living in them…While they continue in their rebellious and resistant state, they should be given the opportunity to hear the Gospel in as courteous a way as possible. But they should not be heavily occupied lest, fearing that they will be swamped by Christians, they become even more resistant."[13]

We do not abandon those who are content, we sow. We are always to seek openings and opportunities the Lord may be orchestrating, but when we do not see open doors, we continue to live as Christ has called us to live, as children of God. God is consistent in His love for His creation and children. There is no ebb and flow with His concerns and care. He simply adjusts his methods for timely seasons. We are to be building relationships regardless. We are to be pouring out love regardless. We are to be consistent with our new nature.

Conclusion

In short, our job is to love others through the ups and downs, to be faithful friends in the good times and the bad, and to be alert and listening to the Holy Spirit at the moment chaos opens the door for the gospel. Once a person decides to follow Christ, we do not stop as if we have bagged a prize; it is then that our love and friendship are the most important to the person. It is in the blackest night that a candle is most useful, when a person is moving from the kingdom of darkness into the kingdom of light, becoming all that God intended the person to be.

Love steadily, be faithful, and keep your eyes open. Your moment to partner with God to transform a human soul may be right around the corner.

---

[1] The number of those responding varied throughout the thirty-nine items on the survey, from 1879 to 2600.

[2] Stetzer, Ed. *Planting New Churches in a Postmodern Age.* (Nashville, TN: B&H Publishing Group, 2007, 336 pages), 130.

[3] Kimball, Dan. *They Like Jesus but not the Church: Insights from Emerging Generations.* (Grand Rapids, MI: Zondervan, 2007, 272 pages), 238

[4] Arn, Win and Arn, Charles. *The Master's Plan for Making Disciples.* (Monrovia, CA: Church Growth Press, 1982. 176 pages), p. 46.

[5] McIntosh, Gary L. *Growing God's Church: How People are Actually Coming to Faith Today,* (Grand Rapids, MI: Baker Books, 2016, 192 pages), 157

[6] From *"Street Level Evangelism: Where is the Space for the Local Evangelist?"* by Michael Parrott, *Acts Evangelism,* Spokane, WA, 1993, pp. 9-11.

[7] Breen, Mike. *Building a Discipling Culture* (3DM International publishing, 2017, 300 pages)

[8] *The Holy Bible: English Standard Version.* (2016). (Jn 6:44). Wheaton, IL: Crossway Bibles.

[9] *The Holy Bible: English Standard Version.* (2016). (Rom 2:4). Wheaton, IL: Crossway Bibles.

[10] Hunter, George G. *The Apostolic Congregation: Church Growth Reconceived for a New Generation.* (Nashville, TN: Abingdon Press, 2009, 141 pages), 77.

[11] Green, Michael. *Evangelism in the Early Church.* (Grand Rapids, MI: Eerdmans, 2003. 474 pages), 282.

[12] Hunter, George G., III. *Go: The Church's Main Purpose* (Nashville, TN: Abingdon, 2017, 164 pages), 28.

[13] McGavran, Donald A. and C. Peter Wagner (editor). *Understanding Church Growth* (Third Edition). (Grand Rapids, MI: Eerdmans, 1990, 332 pages), 261-262.

About the Author

Lance C. Hahn has been the Senior Pastor of Bridgeway Christian Church in Roseville, California, since 1997. He received his M. Div from Western Seminary, Portland, Oregon, and is currently pursuing a D.Min at Talbot Theological Seminary. He is the author of two books, *How to Live in Fear: Mastering the Art of Freaking Out,* and *The Master's Mind: The Art of Reshaping Your Thoughts.* He has participated in many podcasts, written numerous articles, spoken at conferences, and served as an adjunct professor.

GREAT COMMISSION
RESEARCH JOURNAL
2020, Vol. 12(1) 55-65

A MISSIONAL OUTREACH MODEL IN THE CZECH REPUBLIC, A POST-CHRISTIAN, SECULAR CULTURE

Petr Činčala

Andrews University, Berrien Springs, Michigan, USA

Abstract

The Czech Republic is one of the most secular countries in the world. Moreover, the church has not been growing over the last few decades. This case study presents the church planting efforts in the city of Liberec, focusing on an outreach center started by a small number of Christians with the goal of sharing Christ's love in culturally relevant ways. The initial efforts led to a family-centered activity center with many programs that helped develop personal relationships, trust, and open doors to share the gospel. An English class and gospel choir have been at the center of the outreach, but many other activities have been initiated according to the various needs that the leaders saw. This culturally sensitive approach to sharing Christ's love has led to the formation of a small church.

During the 1970s and 1980s, the communist Czechoslovakian government permitted Christians to meet, pray, and worship together. However, this "freedom" was merely a cover, designed to show the

Western world how "open" the country was. The reality was, however, that while Christians had the theoretical ability to meet and pray together, they could only do so in fear, as spies were often among those who would come to such meetings, and their presence could have grave consequences for anyone seen as a threat to the government.

How is it that this was the spiritual climate in the country where the Reformation started and where a strong Protestant presence continued for centuries...the country of the Hussites, the Brethren, the Moravians, and the Anabaptists? Despite this rich history, the process of de-Christianization began as early as the 17th century, when various Reformation efforts were defeated by force. More than three centuries later, the Communists were well aware of the advanced secularization within Czechoslovakia; they took full advantage of it, waiting to victoriously celebrate the burial of the Church.

The Christian church experienced a rebirth after the Velvet Revolution in 1989 when the Communist regime collapsed. Crowds began attending evangelistic meetings, and numerous baptisms were celebrated. However, those days quickly passed, and within half a decade, Christian passion had quieted once again. Despite the new freedom and possibilities that the Velvet Revolution had brought, people gradually drifted away from the churches in greater numbers than ever before. At the turn of the century, mainstream churches lost 30% to 50% of their adherents (Figure 1).

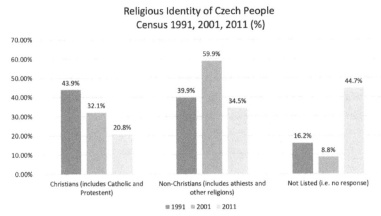

Figure 1. *Changes in Religious Identity in the Czech Republic, 1991-2011 (Český statistický úřad [Czech Statistical Office], 2014, p. 5).*

This period brought to light the harsh reality of how irrelevant Christianity and the church had become to Czech culture. Yet, it also provided an opportunity for the church to rethink its role and mission. Because of this, I chose to complete my PhD (from Andrews University in Berrien Springs, Michigan) focusing on a proposed strategy for mission work. Once approved, this proposal was followed by mission work in the field, testing various ways to expand God's Kingdom in this secular, resistant environment. While the below model had a vague structure before implementation, much of its precision developed in response to people's needs as the work progressed.

Initial Findings

My initial research (Cincala, 2002, p. 239–248) indicated that the Czech people were not as irreligious as they appeared in official polls. Whereas 60% of the Czechs claimed no formal profession of faith, 99% of the studied Czechs believed in a higher power and were not necessarily opposed to spiritual faith. Thus, more accurate statements regarding Czechs' beliefs might be summarized as, "People doubt the importance of the church, not faith," or "For the majority of atheists, God is not an alien concept; however, the way in which the church presents him has left them angry."

A deeper look into Czech history provides some explanation for the attitudes and worldview of Czechs. In the days of John Huss, there was a spirit of criticism directed at the church; that criticism remains part of the national consciousness. However, unlike Huss, most of today's Czechs have stayed away from organized religion. Their faith is marked by intense reservations; the past has left deep wounds on the soul of this nation.

During the communist regime, the pressure for uniformity and the "no religion" policy impacted peoples' self-worth; the government's efforts to discourage individuality and to create a culture where all members were equal undermined people's sense of uniqueness and value. Freedom of thought was limited, particularly in religious matters, and the fear of what others might think kept people away from the church. The critical spirit that has long permeated Czech thinking led many to doubt the value of religious institutions. After the Velvet

Revolution, the gap between church and society grew wider, and by the second half of the 1990s, disillusionment with organized Christianity had built a strong wall separating people from churches. Faith gradually became a completely private matter, and by the time the 2011 census was conducted (as shown in Figure 1), 45% of the population was not willing to identify with a religion.

The Christian Church in general (and especially the Catholic Church) was viewed as like other public institutions, an organization lacking relational elements such as love, trustworthiness, and friendship. Moreover, the church was not able to answer many questions, specifically concerning controversial issues important to the Czech people, such as questions concerning the counter-reformation, the church's part in foreign occupation, the church's role in wars and outrage, the church's claims for restitution, and the church's reputation for wanting power and control. Additionally, the church was perceived as an institution that was constantly asking for sacrifice, be it through money, volunteer work, or in other ways. It was often associated with the loss of freedom, happiness, friends, a sense of self, comfort, and, to some degree, even the loss of peace. It would take time and effort to win back the confidence of the Czech people; the bias against the church had grown too strong. For an increasing number of non-believers, the church had stopped mattering (Cincala, 2005, p. 172).

For that reason, I developed a strategy for reaching Czech people—a method that would take into consideration the context of both the culture and the existing churches. Without plausible bridges of communication, God's tremendous love and desire to save lost people would not make sense in the Czech atheistic worldview.

Launching an Outreach Center

I was born in Czechoslovakia in 1970 and moved to the United States in 1994 to study at Andrews University. After completing my degree, I returned to Czechoslovakia—by that time, known as the Czech Republic. In 2003, I stepped away from formal ministry as a pastor and began working as a missionary in the field. It was during this period that I entered into a time of searching, prayer, and waiting (see Phase 1, Figure 2). My wife and I, along with a small group of women from our church, prayed for several years about how to reach people in our hometown of Liberec. However, we did not know what kind of ministry would be effective and appropriate. Through providential circumstances, we were offered rental of a facility in downtown Liberec. Within this space, we dreamed of bringing together people from all facets of life. The newfound freedoms in the post-communist Czech Republic had created divides, and we desired to create a space connecting young and old, rich and poor, disabled and healthy, politicians and common citizens. Thus, the Generations Center was born. Various ways of reaching people and growing community connections were explored, leading to our purpose statement, "To build healthy relationships, foster personal growth, and live better lives."

The following thirteen years (2006–2018) were filled with various outreach activities, as well as working with children, youth, families, and senior citizens (see Phase 2, Figure 2). The Center became a place where mothers and fathers could spend time with their children, where children attended preschool, and where various interest clubs, leisure activities, and programs took place. People came because their friends invited them or because they had heard positive things about the Center from those around them. The small Christian leadership team was to the growing numbers as "salt" is to the "soup" of life. The work progressed through simply loving people, mingling with them, building relationships, and entering their networks.

Despite a desire—and several attempts—to speak about God and teach the Bible, for a long time, there seemed to be no interest in such topics from the visitors. Because the Center was incarnational, people did not even know they were attending a "Christian" center. By the time they learned the Center was led by Christians, they felt safe. Often, they shared their fear of being pushed or imposed upon by the church. They simply needed more time (see Phase 3, Figure 2). Thus, we simply continued building relationships and serving the community, waiting until the time was right to share the good news of Jesus.

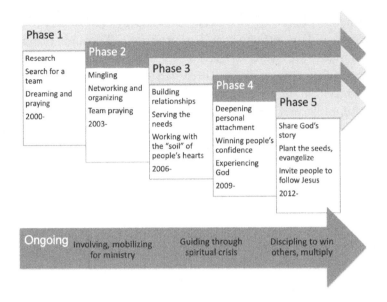

Figure 2. *Phases of mission, with each phase building on the previous.*

Gospel Generation Choir

The Gospel Generation Choir was an initiative of the Generations Center, born out of an adult English class in early 2007. Five students, all on maternity leave, enjoyed spending time with their English teacher, who loved music. They thought that singing songs in the style of the movie "Sister Act" would be a fun idea. These five students invited their friends to join. Although most of these women claimed to be atheists, they did not mind singing Gospel songs in English (their second language). Over time, the group grew numerically and became a close-knit community. They would meet once a week for two hours, bringing their children, sometimes spouses, and spend time together, talking and singing beautiful, heart-touching songs, all while worshipping God—often without realizing it (see Phase 4, Figure 2).

In the early days of the Gospel Generation Choir, we were inexperienced and unprepared for the many hurdles we would encounter. Before one performance, we arrived at the venue to discover there was no sound system in place. I could not help but smile as I told the group, "This is what I call trouble!"

There is a well-known adage in Czech that says, "Every atheist prays when in trouble." On this occasion, we were desperately in need of prayer. So, I said to the group, "Did you know that God has a special P.R. interest in listening to the prayers of atheists and answering them? Can you please pray with me, since God knows I am already a believer?" The group laughed, knowing I was joking to some degree, but they prayed. And while they knew that they did not possess a special "in" with God, there was no denying that things happened, and God moved—even if the choir members did not want to admit it was Him. In this case, we were able to deliver a quite moving performance *without* a sound system, using only one microphone and speaker to amplify our small cassette tape player.

Over time, members would bring prayer requests to the group, and a brief conversational prayer was spoken, or a song was sung in a prayerful spirit, thinking of that particular situation. Again, while many of these prayers were brought before the Lord in a spirit of desperation (that is, with no true belief that God was even real), there was no doubt that God was working in the lives of these choir members. Although many of them were not ready to go to church or study the Bible in the open, their hearts were soaking up God's love through singing, their interactions with other people, kind words, and prayer.

Since its conception, the Gospel Generation Choir has grown to be the largest Gospel choir in the country. The choir has performed more than 200 concerts in public spaces, church buildings, senior homes, weddings, and various other locations. The singers, as well as countless people around them, have experienced God's presence and have learned more about His providence. The choir forms a circle and prays before each performance, and often during rehearsals (see Phase 5, Figure 2). Along the way, some of the members have been baptized, creating a beautiful opportunity for the choir to function as a spiritual family. A handful of people even joined the local church plant (see Ongoing, Figure 2), and made a commitment to serve God in various functions of the outreach, utilizing their spiritual gifts.

Against all odds, 20 years after the Velvet Revolution in 1989, spirituality was present and blossoming amidst the secular society! People have sought to connect with a higher power. They desired to grow personally and to live in harmony. The challenge is no longer to

engage people in spirituality, but to connect secular people with the
loving God, their Creator, and teach them to accept the authority of
His Word (Cincala, 2010).

Today, the Gospel Generation Choir continues to meet; in fact,
the original choir has grown so that there are now three choirs in the
Czech Republic, in Liberec, Jablonec, and Zelezny Brod. The children
of the founding choir members are now old enough to join the choir
and sing along. There is also a choir for senior citizens, called Matylda
a Tylda, which is an offshoot of the original Gospel Generation Choir.
Every time I return to the Czech Republic to visit, I meet with the
leaders for reflection and encouragement. Although the choirs are
quite diverse—made of people with different understandings of
spirituality—the positive Gospel values such as mutual respect,
support, and love for one another have prevailed.

The spirit of community has grown strong, allowing people to
develop a sense of belonging. All the members have been on a journey,
each at a different stage as they pushed forward at their unique pace.
Various activities have impacted members of the community in
different ways, such as one of the Gospel Generation Choir's more
recent Christmas concerts which included the participation of several
black Gospel singers from the United States (Figure 3,
https://youtu.be/CZzOwxwv1vc); all the participants sensed God's
powerful presence (Figure 3).

Figure 3. *The Gospel Generation Choir, a Part of the Missional Outreach
Model.*

In addition to the Gospel Generation Choir, there have been many other ways the Generations Center has worked with people, meeting their needs, and connecting with them relationally. The whole process, however, has been different from what the church plant leaders had expected concerning ministry. Both those who came to the Center out of curiosity and those who have regularly attended some activity of their choosing have been able to be part of a small community that somehow responded to their level of spiritual interest, whether it be latent and hesitant or deeper and engaged.

Those who would never attend explicitly religious activities have been able to become part of a community with believers. The different groups and activities that the Generations Center offered has allowed them to experience God, whether they realized it or not (see Figure 4). In this way, belonging is preceding believing (Rice, 2002); that is, these people belong to a community before, and perhaps long before, they believe in its Leader. People have the freedom to stay at their current level of commitment or move to the next level.

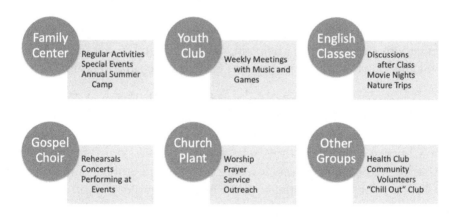

Figure 4. *Relational groups within the spiritual foster family of the Generations Center.*

This model has allowed people to be part of a community, a sort of relational or spiritual foster family. For example, English courses for senior citizens started in 2006. The seniors met regularly, determined to learn a new language. Very soon, however, these people realized that the Center offered much more than merely English courses. They were inspired by their teacher to connect with and support each other. Instead of dropping the class and being discouraged if they did not make any significant progress in learning, they remained involved in the class, some even seven years later, because the English class met their deeper needs. At the same time, they could join other activities, meetings, or events and be exposed to the loving, Christian spirit of the Center. With few exceptions, it took several years for most people to reach a point of starting to believe in the Christian God. However, it did not take long for them to learn that they had a "pastor" who would pray for them or a friend who cared for them, someone whom they could count on in time of need.

This level of connection was especially true for the groups engaged in the fourth phase of mission and beyond. Countless stories related to other ministries could be described here, including summer camps with families, work with youth, and the launch of a national campaign supporting healthy marriage. These ministries each provided space to meet with people, minister to their needs, allow them to experience God's love, and win their confidence. In this missional work with secular people, the receptivity of people to relationships, to a positive emotional environment, and to participating in meaningful services (such as volunteering in the community) was underlined again and again.

Once relationships were built and cherished (Phases 4–5), people were more open to God. They may not have been open to coming to evangelistic meetings or attending Bible studies, but they looked forward to Christian concerts, festivals, rehearsals, and art sessions. They enjoyed watching Christian movies, listening to Christian stories, and singing Christian songs. Interestingly, the English language was often more appropriate for these, because, in the Czech language, religious words are filled with negative connotations; for many Czech people, religious words feel almost as if they are taboo. Speaking them in English gives new life and brings new connotations to the same concepts.

Since its conception in 2002, the Generations Center has borne much fruit. The Gospel Generation Choir experienced its first baptism in 2009, and 20 or so more people were baptized before I left in 2014. In 2018, the nascent church stopped renting the building used as the Center in order to focus on the programs and ministries that the group felt God wanted them to prioritize. Moreover, due to COVID-19, the Liberec choir has not been able to meet for many months; as a result, one of the choir members organized weekly home church worship meetings for the choir members to attend.

This missional outreach model has fostered spiritual healing of the wounds in the Czech psyche as described at the beginning of this article. It has also been a part of a national shift concerning the Christian faith. This missional outreach model demonstrates a culturally relevant and indigenous expression of Christianity in one of the most secular contexts one can presently encounter.

References

Český statistický úřad. (2014). *Náboženská víra obyvatel podle výsledků sčítání lidu.* (Czech Statistical Office. [2014]. *Religious faith of the population according to the results of the census.*) Retrieved from https://www.czso.cz/documents/10180/20551795/17022014.pdf/c533e33c-79c4-4a1b-8494-e45e41c5da18?version=1.0

Činčala, P. (2002). A theoretical proposal for reaching irreligious Czech people through a mission revitalization movement. *Dissertations, 24*. Retrieved from https://digitalcommons.andrews.edu/dissertations/24

Činčala, P. (2005). Church revitalization after the Velvet Revolution in the Czech Republic. *Faculty Publications, 16*. Retrieved from https://digitalcommons.andrews.edu/world-mission-pubs/16

Činčala, P. (2010). Shall thou reincarnate or not? A quest for spirituality among Czech "irreligious" people. *Faculty Publications, 17*. Retrieved from https://digitalcommons.andrews.edu/world-mission-pubs/17

Činčala, P. (2013). Mission to a secular city: The value of research for reaching the unreached. *Spectrum, 41*(1), 47–53.

Činčala, P. (2014, September). Witnessing in the Czech Republic: Not "business as usual." *Adventist World*, 20–21.

Rice, R. (2002). *Believing, behaving, belonging: Finding new love for the church.* Roseville, CA: The Association of Adventist Forums.

About the Author

Petr Činčala, MSW, MDiv, PhD, serves as the Director of the Institute of Church Ministry and the Director of the Doctor of Missiology Program at Andrews University's Seventh-day Adventist Theological Seminary.

GREAT COMMISSION
RESEARCH JOURNAL
2020, Vol. 12(1) 67-92

NARCISSISTIC PASTORS AND THE MAKING OF NARCISSISTIC CHURCHES

Darrell Puls

Gather 4 Him Christian College, Kennewick, Washington, USA

Abstract

Can churches take on the pathological behaviors associated with narcissism through the influence of a narcissistic pastor? While there is a large body of literature on narcissistic individuals, and a smaller body of research into narcissistic organizations, there is little research on the prevalence of toxic narcissism in clergy and little to none on narcissistic churches. This paper is written from the perspective of currently available research and the author's experience in working with churches suffering from severe internal conflicts in which both the pastor and church evidenced toxic levels of narcissism. The intent is to increase awareness, open a dialogue and spur research into the phenomenon of narcissistic clergy and how they influence their churches.

The Narcissist Pastor and the Makings of the Narcissist Church

There are claims that our culture has become increasingly narcissistic. According to Zondag and van Uden (2014), one of the earlier measurements of societal narcissism came in a 1950 study where 50% of teenagers considered themselves to be important; that figure by

1980 had risen to 80%. What might it be today, some 40 years later? The proliferation of camera phones and social media has led to what might be called a narcissistic selfie epidemic (Goldberg, 2017) since narcissistic people are taking more selfies than less narcissistic people (Scion, 2019). Magazines with titles such as *Me* and *Us* proliferate.

Pastors emerge from the entire spectrum of economic and cultural backgrounds as those in any other profession and may have socially undesirable personality traits that are found in the broader population, a manifestation of the sinful condition of humans. What happens when extreme levels of narcissism and religiosity are found in an individual?

Foundational to this paper is an understanding of narcissism in general. Narcissism has been associated with terms such as selfish, egotistical, self-centered, self-absorbed, superiority complex, and so on. Narcissistic tendencies vary in strength but tend to become more difficult to deal with as they increase in intensity.

Every human being has narcissistic tendencies that each person expresses differently. At the lowest end of the spectrum are simple human needs for acceptance, recognition, relationships, and community. People with extremely high narcissism might be diagnosed by licensed mental health providers as having Narcissistic Personality Disorder, (NPD) a psychological disorder; however, extreme levels of narcissism may exist in an individual regardless of a formal diagnosis.

This paper will focus on the behaviors of people with very high levels of narcissism, commonly termed narcissists. Narcissism that is outwardly expressed in interpersonal contexts may be called toxic or malignant narcissism because of the negative and destructive behaviors that accompany it.

Emotions drive behaviors. In general terms, the toxic narcissist experiences fewer key human emotions: empathy, compassion, and love. In their place are envy, fear, and even rage. While the term narcissist is generally thought to mean an overabundance of self-love, the near opposite may be more accurate: they fear they may be perceived as broken or worthless, a fear which may fuel shame. To hide this fear and fulfill a strong need for admiration, they create grandiose fantasies about their great achievements, many of which may be greatly exaggerated or exist only in their imagination. This grandiosity stems from the belief that they are superior to most others and should be recognized as such, often without the achievements that such recognition would require. They see themselves as special, entitled, and unique, and tend to believe they can only be understood by, or should associate with, other special or high-status people. Exercising power and control over their environment and everyone around them is a coping mechanism for dealing with their fears of exposure.

Lacking empathy, they tend to refuse to forgive even the slightest offense, real or imagined. The lack of empathy also allows them to manipulate and exploit others for their own purposes and to discard them when no longer useful. They are often envious of others or believe that others are envious of them (Adapted from DSM5, Diagnostic Criteria 301.81).

These characteristics are not fully descriptive, nor are they simply superficial, external behaviors; they describe the toxic narcissist at the very core of his being: nonempathic, arrogant, entitled, power-centric, exploitative, dishonest, envious, paranoid, and angry. From the perspective of a mental health professional, such behaviors are pathological and become almost untreatable because "the narcissist does not believe there is a problem, let alone that he or she is the problem" (Narcissistic Personality Disorder Statistics). Underneath it all, the narcissist fears that he may be perceived as weak, unworthy, ugly, and broken beyond repair. The paradox is that his ego is so brittle that he cannot even contemplate the idea that there might be something wrong with him; doing so may be the equivalent of death and is to be avoided at all costs (Puls 2020).

Various types of narcissists exist. The most visible are the "grandiose" or overt narcissists. They tend to be extraverted, grandiose, aggressive, entitled, manipulative, and may "place themselves above the bounds of social conventions" (Kealy & Rasmussen 2010, p. 356). While there may be a generalized tendency to see all narcissists as being the same, they are not. The second group is termed covert or vulnerable narcissists. These people tend to be introverted, self-effacing, shame-based, and extremely sensitive to any form of criticism. Both types crave recognition and honor but express their needs differently (Kealy & Rasmussen 2010, p. 359). These differences will be explored in more detail later.

Narcissism is rarely studied in the clergy. Some research focuses on levels of "healthy" or functional narcissism. Zondag and colleagues concluded that more than 80% of the pastors they studied in Poland and the Netherlands scored high to very high in what they termed benign or non-pathological narcissism (Zondag et al., 2009), a narcissism that does no harm. According to that study, these pastors can direct their narcissistic needs in positive directions. The Barna research organization confirmed that narcissism runs high in pastors through self-image questions, concluding that 90% of American pastors scored themselves as excellent to above average preachers and teachers (Barna Group, 2000). As in the Zondag (2009) study, most of these men and women channel their narcissistic needs in positive ways and do little to no harm and even much good.

The focus of this paper is on the two basic types of toxic narcissists, overt narcissists (who tend to be extroverted) and the covert narcissists (who tend to be introverted). The overt (extraverted) narcissists tend to be high energy, charming, intelligent, and full of ideas, but also full of themselves. The covert (introverted) narcissists, also known as vulnerable narcissists, proclaim their merits, but at a much lower volume. Covert narcissists are noted for emotional fragility, which "translates into a need for a target onto which to shift blame, because of their entrenched inability to take responsibility" (Durvasula, 2019, para. 8). As a nondenominational church consultant, I have interacted with many of both types of narcissistic pastors. However, they all saw themselves as victims of ungrateful church members who did not appreciate how blessed they were to have them leading their congregations. Knowing I was there because of problems in their churches, those who show overt narcissistic tendencies have tended to be somewhat hostile towards me. The covert narcissists have tended to be more welcoming and friendly, self-effacing but also clearly pleased when complimented. Since I am responsible for analyzing ongoing problems in their churches, covert narcissists have complained with resignation that a generalized rejection was their cross to carry as pastors. Both types accuse their staffs of incompetence and sabotage. They claim that staffers, including associate pastors, need constant supervision and correction. Their congregations had welcomed them warmly but now have been actively undermining them. The pastors had considered leaving but decided to stay; Jesus suffered, and so must they. One proclaimed that Jesus was only crucified once, but this was his third personal crucifixion.

One of the more difficult realities to accept is that narcissists may intentionally create chaos around them. However, a chaotic work environment was a common staff complaint. According to Dodson (2018), chaos is a hallmark of the narcissist at work, within a family, and in romantic relationships. Whether intentional or not, creating chaos and confusion around them and watching as others struggle to understand and regain some manner of control gives them a sense of superiority and control.

Research on narcissism and religiosity is limited but revealing. Narcissism correlates positively with external but passive religious coping (Cooper & Pullig, 2006) in which the individual and God both take passive rather than active roles in dealing with troubles (Zondag & van Uden, 2010). The narcissist waits for God to intervene, but God is nowhere to be found and so the narcissist is on his own. Further, narcissism negatively correlates with internalized or intrinsic religiosity (Watson et al., 1984), a dimension of religiosity which measures how much a person values the beliefs of that religion. People high in intrinsic religiosity use their beliefs as a guide to live by. Their entire approach to life is framed by their religious beliefs. (Gellman & Turner, 2013).

Feelings of entitlement, a characteristic of both overt and covert narcissists, are positively correlated to expressions of anger towards God (Grubbs & Exline, 2014) and negatively related to willingness to forgive others (Exline et al., 2004), an essential aspect of following Christ (Matt. 6:15). Several studies indicate that narcissists never forgive because they become almost addicted to ruminations of revenge. Siassi (2007) writes, "Nursing a grudge is an attachment to painful affect. . . The attachment is so deep that it informs the subject's identity; the painful affect must be constantly renewed" (1430).

This means that the narcissistic pastor may lead a double life. Pastoral ministry requires pastors to provide empathy, compassion, care, understanding, and forgiveness, all of which the narcissistic pastor does not generally experience but must learn to effectively mimic. At home, out of the public eye, they may be domineering, emotionally abusive, deceitful, and even sexually violent. This naturally creates tensions that might be exposed.

Details of some of my other experiences with narcissistic pastors can be found elsewhere (Puls, 2020), but a basic understanding of pastoral narcissism is necessary for understanding how narcissism can affect a church. First, narcissistic pastors can be highly charismatic, which often enables them to be hired. Charisma often characterizes their public persona, but the narcissistic pastors' staff, board, and family may experience a side that the congregation rarely sees, a person who is arrogant, entitled, controlling, vindictive, manipulative, paranoid, dishonest, unethical, boastful, domineering, self-pitying, and rageful. It is the church staff and his family who are the most common victims. Since the narcissist will rarely accept blame for things gone awry, they can be sadistic when a scapegoat is needed to blame whether at home or in the church (Soleil, 2018).

Narcissists require constant external admiration to be reassured of their self-esteem. The position of pastor would be quite attractive to those who crave such admiration, as it is central to the drama of worship and religious exercise. It offers continuous gratification through telling people how to live with holy writ for a guide, being an integral part of the joys and tragedies of life, being told people's deepest fears and darkest secrets, being sought out for advice and counseling, and being invited to banquets and intimate dinners as the honored guest. Such glory and power might seem quite attractive to a narcissist. Recognition by others is the air they breathe, their "narcissistic supply;" when they do not receive this, they perceive the experience as a personal rejection (a *narcissistic injury*), which may result in an irrational reaction (Bezuidenhout & Wharren, 2013).

Clergy are expected to act compassionately, keep secrets in confidence, listen deeply to confessions of sin, be honest and even transparent – all of which are contrary to the nature of the narcissist. These norms tend to crumble under the stresses of paranoia and feeling unappreciated. Their biggest secret may be that they see God as a rival to be diminished in favor of their own superior qualities (Capps, 2009). However, the culture of politeness found in most churches inhibits truthful conversation (Isaacs, 1999) and requires parishioners to regularly compliment the pastor whether the compliment is earned or not (Godkin & Allcorn, 2011).

Pastors are expected to be humble and spiritually mature so that others might seek them out for guidance. Humility and religiousness are dimensions of the self and are tightly connected, perhaps inseparable. Perhaps the simplest definition of humility is placing God and others above oneself in importance, loyalty, and action. Humility, however, also requires honesty in sharing doubts and questions of faith. The vulnerable narcissist might hint at this, but it is always accompanied by a story of overcoming. The overt narcissist is unlikely to express anything that might indicate vulnerability.

It can safely be concluded that true narcissists know little to nothing about humility, let alone practice it. Interestingly, the narcissists' extrinsic religiosity (religious behavior for the rewards it brings) reflect a religion "they believe that they believe," but it remains forever external and unattainable (Lowicki & Zajenkowski, 2017). If that is the case, and if deep spirituality cannot exist without humility, then whatever spirituality the narcissist pastor exhibits may have little meaning (Rowatt et al., 2014).

Behind the narcissistic façade of care and compassion is a vacuum where the self should be. Kealy and Rasmussen (2012) state there is no real self underneath what they term the "psychological exoskeleton of narcissism." I argue that this is both too harsh and an overstatement. There may still be a deeply wounded human being inside coping in the only way it knows how.

The Making of the Narcissist Church

Narcissists strive for dominance and absolute control of their environment (Johnson et al., 2019). I posit that the narcissist pastor will begin remaking the church into his own image as soon as he arrives.

According to Godkin and Allcorn (2011), "Dysfunctional individual narcissistic leader behaviors are translated into organizational or group beliefs and behaviors through contagion" (p. 62). By contagion they mean the transmission of a dangerous condition through close contact. The implication is that the narcissism of the pastor is contagious and may be transmitted to the congregation through routine close contact.

To understand how this works one must first consider what makes a church vulnerable to narcissistic seduction.

Raising One's Self-Esteem

Christian tradition unequivocally affirms that humility is a virtue. The Jewish scriptures presented humility as a virtue, but Christian scripture and subsequent Christian thought put humility at the center of the moral life of the Christian. There exists a paradox, however. As the Church gained power and wealth, it succumbed to the temptation to glorify itself through pageantry and the power of its wealth. Though Protestantism initially rejected the external pageantry of the Roman church, it can be argued that it has now yielded to the temptation of self-glorification. One need only examine the showpiece auditoria costing millions of dollars that are the new icons of Christian church success. The tension between humility and American notions of success may be irreconcilable.

People tend to find their self-esteem enhanced by the organizations to which they belong. One study examined "...the proposition that group memberships are an important social resource that enhances self-esteem. Specifically, we examined the hypothesis that identification with multiple important social groups provides a basis from which to draw psychological resources to boost personal self-esteem" (Jetten at al., 2015, p. 22). The hypothesis was supported. However, humble surroundings are not particularly attractive to those immersed in the North American visions of success, wealth, and power. Most congregants are not wealthy and so attaching themselves to churches which display wealth and power may be attractive. Most people want the most positive identity they can have, and may find it in a church, particularly when the church presents itself in grandiose terms. In my experience as a church consultant, Protestant churches rarely advertise themselves as humble places for humble people, but it seems that many churches want to be something greater than they are. While it is good to strive towards challenging goals, a small Methodist church in rural Nebraska is unlikely to change the world even though this may be claimed as its goal.

How Churches Become Narcissistic

Pastors in many churches come and go. Churches between pastors often experience a sense of drifting without direction (Scharmer, 2009) and are most vulnerable when seeking a new pastor, a period of organizational change that William Bridges terms "the Neutral Zone," a time of ambiguity and uncertainty. The leader is gone; there is no new leader. The longer a church remains in this state of uncertainty, the more agitated their members become (Bridges, 1998). They may begin to demand quick action, which is an invitation to cut corners in recruiting a new pastor. This leaves the pastor-seeking church open to what I term the Charisma Trap.

The Charisma Trap

Humility is one of the hallmarks of the Christian calling, but as mentioned, success brings a paradox. Our culture's definition of success may be incompatible with humility: greatness, riches, power, beauty, and so on. Mike Play of Biola University writes about his pastoral calling, "All of us who call ourselves pastors are in constant danger of abandoning our vocation to be faithful servants of Jesus and His church in order to pursue our own brilliance" (2017, para. 11). Churches between pastors want someone who can lead them into a brighter future, which is exactly what the narcissist may promise them. They want someone charismatic, even spellbinding, as their pastor. Overt narcissists are often noted for their charisma. Their fear of negative evaluation may fuel the drive to self-aggrandize (Ronningstam & Sommers, 2013). A charismatic narcissist may make claims of forthcoming unlimited success. Wanting to believe and be part of something greater than themselves, followers choose to accept what the leader claims, even if it clashes with their past experiences, reason, or the advice of others. The leader's charisma entrances the church members to prioritize his version of truth, even if perceived as strange (Dawson, 2006).

Two fundamental concepts associated with church growth are vision and mission. The vision can be cast in prophetic terms for long-term planning while the mission is generally more clearly stated in measurable terms. Habakkuk 2:1-2 speaks to vision: "I will stand at my watch and station myself on the ramparts; I will look to see what he will say to me, and what answer I am to give to this complaint. Then the LORD replied: 'Write down the revelation and make it plain on tablets so that a herald may run with it'" (NIV). Proverbs 29:18 states, "Where there is no vision, the people are unrestrained" (NASB).

Pastoral candidates must express a vision for their ministry and the church they seek to shepherd. While honest, humble pastors may want to create a vision of hope, the narcissist pastor will be more grandiose, offering a compelling "vision" of how the church, under his leadership, will reach new heights of visibility, fame, and ministry. This visionary boldness is one reason why narcissists are perceived as leaders (Braun, 2017). In my estimation, this energetic vision casting is also a carefully executed plan of seduction.

The period of pastoral search is a period of vulnerability for the church. The honest resumé of a humble candidate is rarely as exciting as the one presented by a narcissistic candidate. The narcissist's resumé is almost always full of impressive entries. Some may be fabrications, including academic degrees never earned, prestigious positions never held, awards never received, and so on. The assumption is that no one will check. There are ways of detecting narcissism in their written application and cover letter (Craig & Amernic, 2011), but few people are aware of them. In my experience, pastoral search teams often have little or no training in the art of ferreting out accurate information on a candidate – they may stop with the listed references rather than digging two or three layers deeper. They also may tend to ask only polite questions of the candidate and references, rather than difficult ones. A small church may not have the resources necessary to conduct a thorough investigation.

A narcissistic candidate may be counting on the search team to not check each claim. For a more humble applicant, it is a matter of deciding which qualities to emphasize and how to present weaknesses in the best light possible. The vulnerable or covert narcissist may also acknowledge his weaknesses, though he may present them as strengths in showing his determination to serve God despite the obstacles. The overt narcissist, however, often believes he has no defects; therefore, there is nothing to minimize (Atlas & Them, 2008). They also tend to have little sense of subtlety ". . .and tend to use powerful, hyperbolic language" (Craig & Amernic, 2011, p. 569). In one large church I worked with, there were more than 200 applications for the Senior Pastor position. Several cover letters included something like, "I know without a doubt that God has called me to Rivers Edge Church. I have prayed about it and have waited upon the Lord, and He has told me that this is where I am meant to be. Together we will take the church to a higher level. I can't wait to get started!" Three or four claimed to have "placed a fleece before the Lord" à la Gideon, and the fleece was dry despite the rain. It is unlikely that God called several to the same position, but it was a way of identifying potential narcissists because of their apparent sense of entitlement and grandiosity (Puls, 2020). In another instance I investigated, a candidate claimed he held a Ph.D. in psychology from a prestigious university and that he had been a lieutenant-colonel Air Force chaplain. The investigation discovered that the university had never heard of him and his Air Force records indicated he had never been an officer.

Wanting to believe and be part of something greater than themselves, followers choose to accept what the leader claims, even if it clashes with their intuition, logic, or the wisdom of others (Johnson et al., 2019). The church with a new charismatic overt narcissist pastor may grow quickly because it is easy for such a pastor to be seen more as a celebrity than a shepherd. However, the nutrients feeding the roots of the church have changed. Chuck DeGroat (2020) argues that the changes tend to be introduced so gradually that they may be unnoticed as the church slowly takes on more and more narcissistic characteristics. The congregants may be quite content with the changes if the church is growing once again (McNeal, 2003).

Narcissist CEOs (including senior pastors) often lead their organizations into decline (Rijsenbilt & Commandeur, 2013). They run out of fresh ideas, they are caught in too many lies, too many people have left from psychological abuse, the organization may be sued for a hostile work environment, and the staff turnover rate is high. There is also a danger of pastoral embezzlement to fill in the difference between his actual compensation and the compensation to which he feels he is entitled; he may pad personal expense reimbursement requests or use the church credit card for personal purchases (Rijsenbilt & Commandeur, 2013). For people to commit fraud, they need to have the opportunity, the motivation, a rationalization, and the belief that they have the power to deceive (Harrison et al., 2018). A small church pastor with a sense of entitlement may have exactly what is needed. Other times the fraud may be more subtle or sophisticated. For example, the church may buy thousands of copies of the pastor's books to increase the sales ranking and royalties (Kellogg, 2014)

Over time, the church begins to take on the characteristics valued and encouraged by the pastor. He may tell the congregation how unique their church is, how special they are, how others view the church as amazing, how he is inundated by other pastors wanting to know his secrets, and even how he is fending off agents trying to sign him to a book contract. These proclamations supposedly confirm the vision that God has given him. The church may then respond by granting the pastor more freedom to self-aggrandize, exert power—and victimize parishioners. If the pastor is charismatic enough and is able to sustain the excitement long enough, followers will place him on an ever-higher pedestal and increase their commitment to follow him.

The church with a covert narcissist as pastor is not as likely to take on these more obvious characteristics of narcissism simply because the signals from the pastor are not as strong. Even so, the church over time is likely to become more and more isolated from other churches and the belief in their own uniqueness may develop, creating a false sense of superiority.

Life Narratives and Identity

We all have life narratives, or stories we tell ourselves about ourselves, and identity emerges from that narrative (Hussink et al., 2016). Churches also have these narratives. An amalgamation of history, fact, wishful thinking, and even fantasy, the narratives are presented as the life story of the church. As the narrative becomes accepted, the parishioners begin to attach their identities to the church's identity (Johansen, 2017). Eventually, the church's new narrative woven by the narcissist pastor may become a story of humble beginnings, overcoming barriers, and spectacular success. The church's narrative is pliable history influencing the current internal discussions about itself, including the proclamation of its uniqueness. Congregants will believe it, proclaim it, and act on it even if it is largely a self-aggrandizing myth (Babińska & Bilewicz, 2018).

Becoming part of a church involves the emergence of a new personal identity shaped by the church's doctrinal statement, practices, and culture. Individual identities may be partially subsumed into the organizational identity of the church, which can be described as the set of beliefs shared between the leaders and those who attend concerning the central, enduring, and distinctive characteristics of the church, including practices, values, mission, and actions that differentiate it from other churches. This shared identity may provide a needed sense of belonging, making those who attend into stakeholders (Scott & Lane, 2000). The church becomes their home, and the pastor is the new authority figure. Personal and organizational identities give motivation to endure difficult times while difficult times tend to strengthen the identity and the relationships that created it (Babińska & Bilewicz, 2018). In this way the church sees itself as legitimate and important (Brown 1997).

The church narrative provides identity and legitimacy for congregants (Hassink et al., 2016). Over time, newcomers are accepted and become embedded within the narrative and internal life of the church. They become "legitimate" because they accept and share the beliefs of the church and other members. Once they are seen as legitimate members, trust is extended to them and they are viewed as successful (Hassink et al., 2016). As newer members become part of the church, the church becomes part of them and their identity (Dukerich et al., 2000). They are invited deeper and deeper into the church culture and may become increasingly isolated from the rest of the world.

The pastor is at the center of all this. In the narcissist church, the pastor places himself on an ever-elevating platform that takes him above the other members. It can become a type of idolatry in the form of "an idealized self-object." Jennifer Dyer (2012) writes in the *Journal of Religion and Health,*

> ...for many Evangelicals and other Christians, the idealized self-object takes the form of a pastor, speaker, or leader. An idealized self-object is a person for whom the patient has deep respect and wishes to emulate. The evangelical subculture has allowed for the emergence of many leaders, as celebrities, playing roles as artists, authors, pastors, and speakers. Some are even actors. The fans

among these celebrities treasure their words and message. The commercialization of Evangelicalism through publishing, recording, and parachurch organizations that create spaces for festivals, concerts, and conferences further aids in constructing celebrity for these evangelical leaders (p. 247).

Control

The narcissist pastor feels compelled to be in complete control and knows that he controls the church if he controls the governing board. Over time he may replace the old leaders with hand-picked replacements who may be more loyal than competent. They become a layer in his shield against outside attacks. With his selected leaders in positions of power, healthier leaders may disengage or leave. The cycle becomes self-perpetuating as new leaders with stronger narcissistic tendencies emerge.

Church size makes a difference. Dunaetz, Jung, and Lambert (2018) in a preliminary study of 67 evangelical church member experiences found that the larger the church the more tolerant it becomes of a narcissist leader. They credit this to declining opportunities of member activism in the policies of the church as it grows, leaving smaller churches with more active members and less tolerance of narcissistic pastors.

Institutional memory is a check against the fabricated narratives of narcissistic organizations (Kleinberg, 2014). However, even as individual memories can be changed (Loftus, 1996), so too can institutional memories be changed via internal and external influences. The history narrative gives shape to current identities while these modified identities reshape interpretations of past traumas (Babińska & Bilewicz, 2018). In other words, the two play off each other in a circle of reciprocity that is perpetually in motion.

Overt narcissist pastors may demand complete and unquestioning obedience, leading the church to develop cult-like characteristics that influence beliefs and values "along a continuum of various states which include paranoia, obsessive compulsive, dramatic, depressive, schizoid, and narcissistic tendencies" (Hunter, 2013, p. 44). The narrative at the heart of their identity story may be used to strengthen the power of the pastor.

The covert or vulnerable narcissist pastor works hard to avoid conflict, criticism, competition, and even striving for achievement while submitting to circumstances; these unspoken norms are projected into the church (Godkin & Allcorn, 2011). This more passive type of church is generally smaller and may also lack sufficient built-in financial restraints and accountability, thus making allowance for abuse. Clear financial control systems can greatly inhibit behaviors that slow or stymie goal achievement and block the tendency of the narcissist pastor to reward himself outside of authorized channels (Jurkiewicz & Giacalone, 2016).

The narcissist pastor will declare transparency in all the church does but will create a tightly controlled internal communication system with clear lines of authority, both within a rigid hierarchical structure (Brauer, 2017). This discourages alternative opinions and inhibits internal cooperation; there are no clear departmental directives towards goals, all of which constrain communication and create barriers to sharing information and open communication (Brauer, 2017), creating a staff culture of isolated free agents shaping their ministries as they wish.

The pastor sets the example of ethicality—and the narcissist pastor is "ethically challenged." As a result, ethical restraints become weakened. The church will believe it is ethical and the narcissist pastor will proclaim ethicality at every turn, but there is a problem: the narcissist is inherently, perhaps pathologically, unethical (Cooper et al., 2016). He simply does not believe that the rules apply to him. Image, however, is a moderating consideration. The narcissist is far more concerned with appearances than reality; thus, the appearance of an ethical organization feeds his narcissism (Godkin & Allcorn, 2011), which in turn increases the incentive to appear ethical while not necessarily being ethical. His rules tend to bend towards flexibility and exceptions that benefit him. Mostly, they go unnoticed by the congregation (Kleinberg, 2014). Overt narcissists tend to believe that the normal rules of conduct, personal boundaries, finances, and even morality do not apply to them and act accordingly, but in secret. When caught, they will deny any wrongdoing and mount multiple defenses pushing blame away. Multiple famous pastors have made headlines when caught with male and female prostitutes, possessing methamphetamines, stealing money from their churches, and one even went to prison for bilking investors out of millions of dollars. Their belief that they are smarter than everyone else gives them the confidence that they will not be caught (Puls, 2020).

Churches are almost always legally constituted corporations and have hierarchical organizational structures. One would expect churches to be different from secular organizations, and most are. In applying organizational research to churches, narcissistic churches have in some ways lost their moral identities and as a result unwittingly find it difficult to behave ethically (Duchon and Drake 2009). They did not become unethical intentionally but because of their self-obsession, sense of entitlement, self-aggrandizement, denial, and rationalizations. While such churches may not have intentionally abandoned their ethics, the result of that gradual and unnoticed abandonment serves to justify anything they do. If narcissistic churches as organizations tend to parallel private corporations, adopting formal ethics standards and programs may not have much effect on behaviors, e.g., Enron.

The church, though having the appearance of success and outreach, is likely to become more isolated in the community. It is now transitioning to what Jerkiewicz and Giacalone (2014) term an "avoidant organization." Godkin and Allcorn (2011) elaborate, arguing that the avoidant organization suffers having adopted the distorted world and organizational view held by its leaders. Shared dysfunctional beliefs prevent learning more productive behaviors while the unproductive behaviors continue. The result may be "a reality distorting outcome that filters reality and inhibits individual, group and organizational learning" (p. 65) with the result it refuses to acknowledge mistakes. It also tends to develop ethically dysfunctional traits, including deception, distrust, and paranoia. Some employees may become dysfunctionally dependent on the pastor while others begin operating as they wish. It is likely that these churches have no effective succession plan should the pastor suddenly become disabled. In the worst cases, there may be inequality, inhumanity, and dictatorial working conditions characterized by harsh, inflexible, and unyielding mindsets coupled with little to no respect towards staff. These characteristics tend to strengthen the longer the narcissist pastor is unchallenged in power. If institutional morals (core values, mission statements) are not reaffirmed regularly or are poorly communicated, and accountability is lacking, exploitation is likely (Kleinberg, 2014).

Even so, in his grandiosity and entitlement, it is likely the narcissist pastor will enthusiastically endorse these affirmations all the while believing they do not apply to him.

Brown (1997) argues in an extensive analysis of organizational narcissism that "collective entities, in the form of groups and organizations, literally have needs for self-esteem that are regulated narcissistically" (p. 303). As people become part of the church, the church becomes part of them in a reciprocal transfusion of culture, personality, and needs (Volkan & Fowler, 2009).

Crossing the Rubicon

There are warning signs the church has crossed from relatively normal narcissism into what might be called Narcissistic Personality Organization (Volkan & Fowler, 2009). In confirmation, Laing and Dunn (2014) argue that organizations can institutionalize a sense of superior identity and legitimacy that encourages narcissistic behavior, particularly in its employees who will believe their organization to be extraordinary and unique. From this comes a belief that the organization is in some sense all-powerful and even omniscient with access to all relevant information – incongruent or contradictory information is summarily rejected. The delusion of superiority allows the organization to be dismissive of other organizations, people and information and treats them with contempt. These ideas may become so embedded in the organizational mindset that they manifest in groupthink.

These organizations (in this case churches) tend to rationalize and endow themselves with claims of righteousness and even some level of sentience as part of their uniqueness. "This anthropomorphism is a concern since it implies that an organization may indeed have the capacity to act and develop a form of personality" (Laing & Dunn, 2014, pp. 61–62; Scharmer, 2009).

Denial

No church is perfect, yet church members tend to conceal or simply deny any disagreeable truths about the churches they belong to (Brown 1997, p. 654), confirming Ten Elshof's (2009) contentions about how Christians are little different from others in having a penchant for self-deception. We believe what we want to believe. If it is believed that the church is highly superior and unique, organizational miscues and mistakes must then be denied or blamed on other people or churches.

Since the narcissist pastor will rarely admit error or failure, the narcissist church will likely follow suit. If concealment is not an option, circumstances, outside forces, or sabotage may be blamed—anything so the fault does not belong to the pastor. If there is no other viable scapegoat, it is not uncommon for the narcissist pastor to blame the church members themselves and demand that they repent and right their wrongs against him.

Uniqueness

Claims of uniqueness require comparison, a "them" that is not "us". This creates an unresolvable dynamic tension between the two. "The pathological form of narcissistic collective self-love inevitably leads to rage against 'them,' that is, against those who fail to be part of 'us' because they differ in some significant way" (Brunner, 2002, p. 124). Churches need members and uniqueness attracts them, so they seek identifiers branding the church as unique. Thus, rebranding churches to promote church growth has become a major industry. Branding and rebranding are legitimate and nothing new. However, a new name and core values mean nothing if they were adopted only to change the church image.

Grandiosity

Grandiosity and uniqueness are normal behaviors for narcissists, who tend to be tone-deaf regarding how others perceive their proclamations. Narcissistic bragging comes naturally, but it is exaggerated and often includes events that never happened. It is no different for the pastors of narcissistic churches. For example, a few years ago a church petitioned the local ministerial association demanding that its pastor become the next leader and strongly implied the results would be greatness for all. The petition failed.

Paranoia/Isolation

The narcissist church will gradually withdraw from associations with other churches and their pastors, though it may not directly reflect the paranoia of its pastor. This will manifest as a sense of superiority over other churches, which then have nothing of value to offer. Instead, other churches and outside ministries may be rejected over real or imagined offenses or inadequacies. Paranoia serves to further isolate the church and may lead to a sense of being persecuted even though there is no evidence for it. If the members feel they are under some form of outside attack they are likely to band more tightly together and add to the overcoming persecution section of the church narrative. Some will leave, but a strong sense of bonding is also likely. Jan Schwarz (2007), in writing about paranoid organizations, states "A paranoid organization is characterized by distrust, anxiety, and a permanent readiness to repel attack. The organization is highly sensitive to all kinds of threats, builds sophisticated control mechanisms and management information systems and constantly searches for the hidden intentions of others." (p. 20).

At the most extreme, the narcissist church can be described as a cult where a warped gospel message proclaims that Truth can be found nowhere else. As the church turns ever further inward, the message of paranoia and isolation grows stronger.

Lack of Empathy

Galatians 6:1–2 requires gentle restoration of church members found to be "in sin," but gentle restoration is not the narcissist way. Violating the norms is an affront to both the church and the narcissist pastor that must not go unpunished. In one church a young woman confessed an affair to the pastor and was told she must confess to the entire church. Obviously repentant, and expecting comfort and forgiveness, she did the following Sunday—and was promptly told to leave and never come back (Puls 2020, p. 163). In this fashion the narcissist church draws its members ever deeper into a cold, rigid, and unforgiving conformity and ruthlessly expels anyone who resists.

As I have seen in multiple churches, people with questions or criticisms will be told privately that they would probably be much happier elsewhere, which is a shaded message to leave and never come back. Even more subtle are the places that begin a whispering campaign against someone that eventually cuts them off from their friends and makes it known that they simply are no longer welcome.

Conformity is enforced in this way.

Little Awareness of External Perceptions

Like the narcissist, the narcissist church will have little awareness of external perceptions. External criticisms can be summarily dismissed because they do not comport with the internal narrative of uniqueness and greatness. The more isolated the church becomes the fewer outside interactions there will be until there are few to none. If the church is narcissistic enough, the members simply do not care what others think about them but are certain that the outside image is wonderful. Even so, the paranoia remains. Distrust and anxiety may predominate. Sensitivity to outside threats is maintained at a constant high level. While never announcing it, the staff and governing board are on a constant war footing as they scan for internal and external threats (Hunter, 2013).

There is an intentional escalation to this phenomenon and it is used to isolate the church and its members into a more cohesive and even cultic group: the leaders proclaim they are all under attack by unidentified outsiders who come with kind words and gestures but with terrible, evil intentions. The result is often tighter unity and deeper isolation.

Rationalization

Andrew Brown (1997) of the University of Cambridge argues that while secular organizations tend to rationalize their less than ethical actions to the media, churches seem more inclined to secretive internal rationalizations. Brown says that policy makers are often more inclined to satisfy their own personal motives and emotional needs than the requirements of their organizations. The result is that decisions are made for egocentric reasons, which then must be justified/rationalized (often un-self-consciously) internally by means of impressive-sounding reasons. The first major rationalizations may be found in the upper strata of leadership: the pastor and his or her most trusted (as far as a narcissist can trust) associates. This becomes possible because organizations, including many churches, allow dark or hidden places to be created where the status quo is in control; there is nothing to see and no questions may be asked. The social order of organizations creates rationalizations that in turn highlight favorable events and obscure or cloak unfavorable events. The result is that memories are controlled and identities are more rigidly fixed.

Brown (1997) aptly summarizes the dilemmas and traps that churches and their members are susceptible to:

> Moral rewards, which an individual accrues as a result of a perceived correspondence between his/her morality and the several aspects of the organization, are similarly associated with positive self-esteem. These rewards encourage the individual to self-aggrandize ("because I am a member of a virtuous or worthwhile organization, I too am virtuous or worthwhile"), to deny moral improprieties and questioning of the individual's social utility ("since I participate in a good organization, my actions must be good"), to rationalize actions ("my actions are prompted by virtuous motives"), to possess a sense of entitlement ("the virtuous should receive"), and to engage in attributional egotism ("since I am good, so are the consequences of my actions"). (Brown, 1997, p. 666).

Church Disintegration

The narcissist, whether overt or covert, is inherently self-destructive. Narcissistic paranoia can lead to church disintegration where the church loses internal cohesiveness and splits into competing or even warring factions. In my experience the triggering event is often a rebellion against the narcissist pastor. As the conflict escalates, each faction may become more and more deeply enmeshed in its own self-righteous truth-story that it uses to justify what would otherwise be unjustifiable acts against competing factions. It can reach the point where inconvenient facts are summarily rejected. The very meaning of words is questioned and distorted to justify the actions of one group towards the others (Glasl, 1999, pp. 104-105). The eventual outcome may by the complete destruction of the church, which this writer recently witnessed in New York.

Conclusion

Stein (2003) argues that extreme organizational narcissism has five attributes:

1. Members will believe their organization to be extraordinarily special and unique. This is not normal pride but is instead highly exaggerated to the point of delusion.

2. A powerful sense of self-aggrandizement and entitlement leads to a kind of unconscious imperialism or an unconscious omnipotence: The organization is all powerful and . . . cannot recognize that anything of value might exist outside its boundaries.

3. The organization believes itself to be omniscient; that is, it has access to all information, both internal and external, that is relevant to the organization and interprets the information correctly.

4. The delusion allows it not only to be dismissive of other organizations, people and information, but also to treat them with a kind of triumphant contempt.

5. These attributes become permanently embedded in organizational functioning (pp. 537–538).

If Stein is correct and the attributes of extreme narcissism become permanently embedded in the church culture, when the pastor leaves, the church may perpetuate its own narcissism by seeking out another narcissist pastor.

References

American Psychiatric Association. (2013). *Diagnostic and statistical manual of mental disorders* (5th ed.). https://doi.org/10.1176/appi.books.9780890425596

Atlas, G. D., & Them, M. A. (2008). Narcissism and sensitivity to criticism: A preliminary investigation: Research and reviews. *Current Psychology, 27*(1), 62–76. https://dx.doi.org/10.1007/s12144-008-9023-0

Babińska, M, & Bilewicz, M. (2018). Self-sacrifice for in-group's history: A diachronic perspective. *Behavioral and Brain Sciences, 41*, 1–12. https://doi:10.1017/S0140525X18001796

Barna Group. (2000). Pastors rate themselves highly. Retrieved from https://www.barna.com/research/pastors-rate-themselves-highly-especially-as-teachers/

Bezuidenhout, C., and Wharren, M. (2013). An analysis of the probable association between narcissistic personality disorder and a rage-type murder event (Part 1). *Pakistan Journal of Criminology; Peshawar (5)*2, 251–273.

Boddy, C. (2015). Organizational psychopaths: A ten-year update. *Emerald Insight*, 2407–2432. www.emeraldinsight.com/0025-1747.htm

Braun, S. (2017). Leader narcissism and outcomes in organizations: A review at multiple levels of analysis and implications for future research. *Frontiers in Psychology, 8*(773). https://www.frontiersin.org/articles/10.3389/fpsyg.2017.00773/full

Brown, A. (1997). Narcissism, identity, and legitimacy. *Academy of Management Review, 22*(3), 643–686. http://amr.aom.org/content/22/3/643.short

Brunner, J. (2002). Contentious origins: Psychoanalytic comments on the debate over Israel's creation. In John Bunzl and Benjamin Bair-Halahmi (Eds.) *Psychoanalysis, identity, and ideology: Critical essays on the Israeli/Palestine case* (107–136). New York: Springer.

Coffee, B. (2014). Entitlement and the Church. Christian Unity Ministries. https://www.christianunityministries.org/?s=entitlement

Cooper, L., Bruce, J., Harman, M., & Boccaccini, M. (2009). Differentiated styles of attachment to God and varying religious coping efforts. *Journal of Psychology and Theology, 37*(2), 134–141.

Cooper, M., Pullig, C., & Dickens, C. (2016). Effects of narcissism and religiosity on church members with respect to ethical judgment, confidence, and forgiveness. *Journal of Psychology and Theology, 44*(1), 42–54.

Craig, R. & Amernic, J. (2011). Detecting linguistic traces of destructive narcissism at-a-distance in a CEO's letter to shareholders. *Journal of Business Ethics, 101,* 563–575.

Dawson, L. (2006). Psychopathologies and the attribution of charisma: A critical introduction to the psychology of charisma and the explanation of violence in new religious movements. *Nova Religio: The Journal of Alternative and Emergent Religions; Chappaqua, 10*(2), 3–28.

Dodgson, L. (2018). Why you should be aware of something called the 'drama triangle' — a manipulative tactic narcissists use to keep you on your toes. *Insider.* https://www.insider.com/drama-triangle-how-narcissists-use-it-to-manipulate-people-2018-10

Duchon, D. and Drake, B. (2009). Organizational narcissism and virtuous behavior. *Journal of Business Ethics, 85,* 301–308. https://doi:10.1007/s10551-008-9771-7

Dukerich, J., Golden, B., & Shortell, S. (2002). Beauty is in the eye of the beholder: The impact of organizational identification, identity, and image on the cooperative behaviors of physicians. *Administrative Science Quarterly, 47*(3), 507–533.

Dunaetz, D., Jung, H., & Lamberts, S. (2018). Do larger churches tolerate pastoral narcissism more than smaller churches? *Great Commission Research Journal, 10*(1), 69–89.

Durvasula, R. (2019). Insecurity, narcissism, and the culture of victimhood. *Psychology Today Online.* https://www.psychologytoday.com/us/blog/guide-better-relationships/201908/insecurity-narcissism-and-the-culture-victimhood

Dyer, J. E. (2012). Loving thyself: A Kohutian interpretation of a 'limited' mature narcissism in evangelical mega churches. *Journal of Religion and Health, 51*(2), 241–255.

Exline, J.J., Baumeister, R.F., Bushman, B.J., Campbell, W.K., & Finkel, E.J. (2004).

Too proud to let go: Narcissistic entitlement as a barrier to forgiveness. *Journal of Personal and Social Psychology, 87*(6), 894–912.

Fernbach, P., Light, N., Scott, S., and Rozin, P. (2019). Extreme opponents of genetically modified foods know the least but think they know the most. *Nature Human Behavior.* https://doi.org/10.1038/s41562-018-0520-3

Gellman, M., & Turner, R. (2019). *Encyclopedia of Behavioral Medicine.* Springer. https://doi.org/10.1007/978-1-4419-1005-9

Giacalone, R.A., & Jurkiewicz, C.L. (2003). Right from wrong: The influence of spirituality on perceptions of unethical business activities. *Journal of Business Ethics, 46,* 85–97. https://doi.org/10.1023/A:1024767511458

Glasl, F. (1999). *Confronting conflict: A first aid kit for handling conflict.* Hawthorne.

Godkin, L., & Allcorn, S. (2011). The narcissistic manager, avoidant organization, and interruptions in organizational learning. *International Journal of Organization Theory and Behavior, 14*(1), 58–82.

Goldberg, G. (2017). Through the looking glass: The queer narcissism of selfies. *Social Media + Society,* (Jan-Mar), 1–11. https://doi.org/10.1177/2056305117698494

Grubbs, J., & Exline, J. (2014). Humbling yourself before God: Humility as a reliable predictor of lower divine struggle. *Journal of Psychology and Theology, 42*(1), 41–49.

Harrison, A., Summers, J., & Mennecke, B. (2018). The effects of the dark triad on unethical behavior. *Journal of Business Ethics, 153,* 53–77.

Hassink, J., Grin, J., & Hulsink, W. (2016). Identity formation and strategy development in overlapping institutional fields. *Journal of Organizational Change Management, 29*(6), 973–993. https://doi.org/10.1108/JOCM-07-2015-0122

Hoffman, B., Strang, S., Kughnert, K., Campbell, K., Kennedy, C., and LiPilato, A. 2013. Leader narcissism and ethical context: Effects on ethical leadership and leader effectiveness. *Journal of Leadership and Organizational Studies 20*(1): 25-37. https://doi:10.1177/1548051812465891

Hunter, M. (2013). The psychosis of organizations. *Contemporary Readings in Law and Social Justice 5*(1), 44–47.

Isaacs, W. (1999). *Dialogue and the art of thinking together.* Currency.

Jackson, R., Wood, C., & Zboja, J. (2013). The dissolution of ethical decision-making in organizations: A comprehensive review and model. *Journal of Business Ethics, 112,* 233–250.

Jetten, J., Branscombe, N., Haslam, S., Haslam, C., et al. (2015). Important group memberships as a source of self-esteem. *PLoS One, 10*(5), 1-30. https://10.1371/journal.pone.0124609

Johansen, T.S. (2017). Me, we and them: Complexity in employee and organizational identity narration. *Tamara - Journal for Critical Organization Inquiry, 15*(1-2), 175–189.

Johnson, E., Kidwell, L., Lowe, D.J, & Reckers, P. (2019). Who follows the unethical leader? The association between followers' personal characteristics and intentions to comply in committing organizational fraud. *Journal of Business Ethics, 154*(1), 181-193. https://doi:10.1007/s10551-017-3457-y

Jurkiewicz, C., & Giacalone, R. (2014). Organizational determinants of ethical dysfunctionality. *Journal of Business Ethics, 136*, 1–12. https://doi:10.1007/s10551-014-2344-z

Kellogg, C. (2014, April 13). Pastor Mark Driscoll's books withdrawn from 180 Christian stores. *Los Angeles Times*. https://www.latimes.com/books/jacketcopy/la-et-jc-pastor-mark-driscoll-books-withdrawn-from-christian-stores-20140813-story.html

Kleinberg, J. (2014). The dynamics of corruptogenic organizations. *International Journal of Group Psychotherapy, 64*(4), 421–443.

Laing, G., & Dunn, B. (2018). Organizational narcissism: A review of the indicators in the major Australian banks. *E-Journal of Social & Behavioral Research in Business, 9*(1), 58–75.

LeMaitre, B. (2017). Science, narcissism and the quest for visibility. *The FEBS Journal, 284*, 875–882. https://febs.onlinelibrary.wiley.com/doi/pdf/10.1111/febs.14032

Loftus, E. & Meacgum, K. (1992). *The myth of repressed memory*. St. Martin's Griffin.

Lowicki, P. and Zajenkowski, M. (2017). No empathy for people nor for God: The relationship between the Dark Triad, religiosity, and empathy. *Personality and Individual Differences, 115*, 169–173. https://doi.org/10.1016/j.paid.2016.02.012

McNeal, R. (2003). *The present future: Six tough questions for the church*. Jossey-Bass.

Play, M. (2017). Pursuing obscurity: A call to pastoral humility. *The Table*. Biola University Center for Christian Thought. https://cct.biola.edu/pursuing-obscurity-call-pastoral-humility/

Puls, D. (2020). *Let us prey: The plague of narcissist pastors and what we can do about it (Rev. Ed.)*. Cascade Books.

Recovery Village. (n.d.). Statistics on narcissistic personality disorder. https://www.therecoveryvillage.com/mental-health/narcissistic-personality-disorder/related/npd-statistics/#gref

Ronningstam, E. & Baskin-Sommers, A. (2013). Fear and decision-making in narcissistic personality disorder—a link between psychoanalysis and neuroscience. *Dialogues Clinical Neuroscience 15*(2): 191–201.

Rowatt, W., Kang, L., Haggard, M., & LaBouff, J. (2014). A social-personality perspective on humility, religiousness, and spirituality. *Journal of Psychology and Theology, 42*(1), 31–40.

Scharmer, C. O. (2009). *Theory U: Leading from the future as it emerges*. Barrett Kohler Schwartz-Salant, N. (1982). *Narcissism and character transformation: The psychology of narcissistic character disorders*. Inner-City Books.

Schwarz, J. O. (2007). Assessing future disorders in organizations: Implications for diagnosing and treating schizophrenic, depressed or paranoid organizations. *Foresight: The Journal of Futures Studies, Strategic Thinking and Policy, 9*(2), 15–26. https://doi:10.1108/14636680710737722

Scott, S., & Lane, V. (2000). A stakeholder approach to organizational identity. *The Academy of Management Review, 25*(1), 43–62.

Siassi, S. (2007). Forgiveness, acceptance and the matter of expectation. *International Journal of Psychoanalysis, 88*, 1423–40. https://doi.org/10.1516/4W17-3154-1T35-T460

Sion, G. (2019). Narcissistic performance, public adoration, and the commodification of reified persona. *Contemporary Readings in Law and Social Justice, 11*(2), 70–75.

Soleil, N. (2018). Narcissists and scapegoats: A comparison of traits and behaviors. https://www.differentbrains.org/narcissists-and-scapegoats-a-comparison-of-traits-and-behaviors/

Stein, M. (2003). Unbounded irrationality: Risk and organizational narcissism at long term capital management. *Human Relations 56*, 523–538.

Valashjardi, A. & Charles, K. (2019). Voicing the victims of narcissistic partners: A qualitative analysis of responses to narcissistic injury and self-esteem regulation. *Sage Open* (Apr 28). https://doi.org/10.1177/2158244019846693

Vazquez, D. (2003). I can't be me without my people: Julia Alvarez and the postmodern personal narrative. *Latino Studies, 1*(3), 383–403. https://doi:10.1057/palgrave.lst.8600042.

Volkan, V., & Fowler, J.C. (2009). Large group narcissism and political leaders with Narcissistic Personality Organization. *Psychiatric Annals, 39*(4): 214–223.

Wallace, H., Scheiner, B., & Grotzinger, A. (2016). Grandiose narcissism predicts willingness to behave badly, without proportional tolerance for others' bad behavior. *Current Psychology: Research and Reviews, 35*(2), 234–243. https://doi:10.1007/s12144-016-9410-x

Watson, P. J., Wood, T., & Morris, R. (1984). Religious orientation, humanistic values and narcissism. *Review of Religious Research, 25*(3), 257–264.

White, Jay. D. 1997. Review of Michael Diamond, *The Unconscious Life of Organizations*. *Public Administration Review, 57*(4), 358–360.

Zondag, H., & van Uden, C. (2014). My special prayer: On self, God, and prayer. *European Journal of Mental Health, 9*(1), 3–19. https://doi:10.5708/EJMH.9.2014.1.1

Zondag, H., & van Uden, M. (2010). I just believe in me: Narcissism and religious coping. *Psychology of Religion, 32*, 69–85. https://doi:10.1163/008467210X12626615185702

Zondag, H., van Halen, C, & Wojtkowiak, J. (2009). Overt and covert narcissism in Poland and the Netherlands. *Psychological Report, 104*, 1–10.

About the Author

Darrel Puls has been a consultant helping churches manage conflicts since 1998. He is Dean of Academics at Gather 4 Him Christian College (Kennewick, WA) and has written two books and several articles on conflict management.

GREAT COMMISSION
RESEARCH JOURNAL
2020, Vol. 12(1) 93-96

BOOK REVIEW

A Guide to Church Revitalization.

By Mohler, Albert, R., Jr., Ed.
Louisville, KY: SBTS Press, 2015.
88pp.
US$4.99.

Reviewed by Dustin Slaton, Campus Pastor at Green Acres Baptist Church–South in Flint, TX and a PhD student at Southwestern Seminary in Ft. Worth, TX. He lives in Flint with his wife and four children.

A Guide to Church Revitalization is number five in a series of "guidebooks" published by SBTS Press. The volume in question is edited by SBTS's President, Albert R. Mohler, Jr., who also penned the opening chapter. The book's chapters are each written by different authors moving systematically from defining the problems to providing solutions and plans for church revitalization.

Mohler begins the book with a general overview of the need for church revitalization. Mohler paints a grim picture of the reality of the church in America. As most churches are plateaued or declining, he implores men and churches to commit themselves to the task of revitalizing dying churches. His hope is to see a passionate "Generation Replant" among church leaders and seminary students, who can revive churches to God's glory.

Kevin Ezell, president of the Southern Baptist Convention's North American Mission Board, describes the resources available through NAMB. He lists church decline issues and explains three ways NAMB comes alongside churches and church leaders to help bring about revitalization: one-day conferences for training pastors in assessing and preparing for revitalization; tools and resources for churches which are geared toward their specific situation; and work with churches, called "legacy churches" to help hand off their resources to a church or group who can develop a healthy church which can move forward in their location.

Dan Dumas, currently a leadership and organizational consultant, writes about the type of person capable and called to revitalization. This chapter gives a brief exposition of the biblical qualifications of a pastor/elder found in 1 Timothy 3. Dumas expounds on the qualifications and points out how they specifically apply to the revitalizing pastor.

Chapter four is by Brian Croft, the Senior Pastor of Auburndale Baptist Church in Louisville, KY. Croft instructs the revitalizer in how to prepare the church for revitalization through assessment. He lists five critical areas to assess. First, the church must discover who truly holds the power in the church. Second, the true leaders of the church must also be identified, to find who the church members will follow. Third, the church must discover its true process for membership so that a better definition of membership can be established. Fourth, the church must assess its willingness to be unified across all demographics so that one group does not control the direction of the church and ostracize others. Finally, the church must determine what the priorities are in worship. If the priorities are personal tastes above the worship of God, changes must be made.

David Prince, pastor of Ashland Avenue Baptist Church in Lexington, Kentucky, makes the case that preaching which elevates, exalts, and expounds the Word of God is central to the task of revitalization. All other strategies will fall short without the clear teaching of God's Word because that Word, the Gospel, is the foundation of the church.

Donald S. Whitney, Professor of Biblical Spirituality at SBTS, focuses on a revival of interpersonal disciplines which will bring spiritual renewal and unity to the congregation. These congregational disciplines include hearing the word, corporate worship, evangelism, serving, giving, fellowship, and prayer.

Tim Beougher, Professor of Evangelism and Church Growth at SBTS and Brian Croft together describe a "road map" to revitalization. They say the two essential keys to this roadmap are faithfulness and survival on the part of the pastor. In order to be faithful to God, the church, and the process, pastors must trust the word, shepherd the people, love all people, pray hard, and celebrate older members of the church. In order to survive the rigorous process of revitalization, pastors must be patient, expect suffering, pick battles wisely, love difficult people, and trust the chief shepherd.

Eric Bancroft, the Pastor of Grace Church in Miami, FL provides the revitalizing pastor with some indicators of success. He says to look for a renewed appetite for the Word of God throughout the church, a culture of discipleship in the church, a passion for evangelism, and unity among the leaders. These elements are rarely seen in a declining church, so their presence will indicate revitalization is taking place.

The book concludes with three chapters of interviews with three pastors, Mark Devers, Brian Croft, and Andrew Davis, who have all led their churches in revitalization. These chapters give the reader an inside look at the process and how it has been different for each congregation. It also provides some insights for pastors who see similarities between their situation and those these pastors experienced.

A Guide to Church Revitalization is an interesting title for this book. In one sense, it is accurate. The book does give basic guidelines and principles for how revitalization can take place in a church. On the other hand, it is not a guidebook at all if the reader is looking for a step-by-step, how-to guide to revitalization. The book, in essence, is a curated selection of key topics essential for church revitalization, gathered for the goal of introducing the topic to a wide range of audiences.

This book succeeds in its goal of *introducing*. Students of the subject of church revitalization will find nothing new in this book, and pastors of healthy churches will find little use or new information in its pages. This book will be most beneficial for those who are helping leaders discover hope for their church. It is a great resource for denominational leaders to provide to pastors and leaders of struggling churches. It is a great book for pastors of struggling churches to give to their leaders so they can begin their own assessment of their church and its future.

As this book is an introductory volume, the best resource in the entire book may be the list of recommended readings on page 84.

GREAT COMMISSION
RESEARCH JOURNAL
2020, Vol. 12(1) 97-100

BOOK REVIEW

Church Planting in the Secular West: Learning from the European Experience.

By Paas, Stefan.
Grand Rapids, MI: William B. Eerdmans Publishing Company, 2016.
304pp.
US$34.00.

Reviewed by Keith R. Sellers, D. Min. candidate in Church Growth and Multiplication, Talbot School of Theology, missionary in Europe with WorldVenture Mission.

Labeling himself a "skeptical advocate" of church planting (3), Stefan Paas presents a missional theology on church planting in the secular West. The text is born out of his theological reflection and direct missional experience in a post-Christian European culture. His ministry expertise is evidenced by two church plants in the Netherlands. Currently he serves as a missiology professor at Vrije Universiteit Amsterdam and the Theological University of Kampen, Netherlands.

In chapter one, Paas describes the classic paradigm of church planting in the Middle Ages, *plantatio ecclesiae*, as planting churches in areas where there was no Christian presence with the proper sequence as evangelism, gathering, and planting (16). He then presents the modern and late-modern evangelical paradigms as rooted in the

Enlightenment, the Reformation, organic church thinking, and church growth theory.

Paas traces a valuable survey of the Christianization of Europe as it relates to church planting (Chapter 1). Paas shows how the Reformation's individualism affected the Pietist movements and eventually evolved to the individual rejection of faith altogether, hence secular Europe. Such a pattern of gradual secularization may repeat itself in American and Asian democracies. The book should have at least mentioned the secularizing effects of Europe's socialist philosophical movements, two tragic world wars, the rise of French postmodern writers, and western materialism. Individualism alone is not responsible for contemporary European secularism.

In the second chapter, *Planting Better Churches*, Paas addresses two popular reasons for church planting in Europe, the failure of traditional churches in evangelizing their country and the need to enrich the overall Christian expression of the nation. Analyzing the ties that the Reformation, Anabaptists, and Pietism had on church planting in Europe from the 16th to the 19th century, Paas again shows how individualist approaches to persuading inquirers to make faith-based decisions evolved to a pervasive, individualized rejection of faith in Europe.

The third chapter, *Planting More Churches*, is perhaps the most controversial chapter. Paas lays out a detailed critique against church growth theory (CGT). Paas unleashes much criticism of the inherent pragmatism of church growth theory (CGT), and accuses its proponents of unknowingly implementing religious market theory (RMT), which he believes will not work in the European setting (129-131). CGT adherents will quickly object, noting that McGavran's thinking is rooted in communication theory, cultural anthropology, and biblical precedents. Paas finds fault with McGavran's view that we need to plant many new churches in order to reach modern Europe (113-114). He accuses proponents of CGT of making church planting equivalent to the gospel. In a slow-to-respond Europe, a church's faithfulness may be defined much differently than in areas where people are quicker to make conversations with new people and convert to new concepts.

Chapter four explores the right conditions and motives for innovative church planting in Europe. The final chapter, *In Defense of Church Planting in Europe*, lists four important reflections on the relationship of church and mission. The author promotes the "communal character of evangelism" which in his mind is most vividly seen in the life of small churches (261-63).

Those seeking field ready methods for church planting among secular people might be disappointed because Paas intends to analyze "reasons and motives for church planting in Europe" (2). John R. Franke commends the work as "providing a missional theology of church planting in the aftermath of Christendom" (xii). While American readers may question the relevance of this work for their continent, Franke warns, "we are surely headed in that direction" (x).

Like other critics of CGT Paas misunderstands the intentions and effects of the homogenous unit principle (HUP). He condemns the HUP in chapter three, but later he states that the reason immigrant churches fail to effectively reach native Europeans is due to the "gap of race and culture" (177). Reducing cultural gaps is precisely what McGavran's HUP is all about. In the last chapter Paas wisely advocates a "greater diversity of churches" in light of recent globalizing trends (252). Strangely, he advises implementing ideas, which are rooted in the homogenous unit concept, and then a few lines later he condemns HUP as "theologically suspect" (252-253). Using Paul's practice of being "all things to all men" as a theological basis, he supports the use of the multi-congregational model to reach different kinds of people within the same parish church (252). Such a model is rooted in the homogenous unit principle. Another helpful strategy, which Paas mentions includes making church planting adjustments to areas with too many of the same kind of churches or with an uneven distribution. He admits that "young congregations are almost always quite homogenous," but he believes that the church must reach out to a wider constituency to avoid the sin of exclusivity (254-255). One new trend unfortunately left out of the last chapter includes the planting of multi-ethnic churches wherein ethnically diverse leaders start with the homogenous goal of being a heterogeneous fellowship.

European churchmen are rightfully offended by the American penchant for grand goal setting, proud self-promotion, and unmitigated pragmatism. Paas believes that some places have "enough churches," but he fails to define exactly what that means in demographics (31). Because North American culture sometimes tends to follow European trends the book serves as a profound warning concerning what difficulties may await the American religious scene.

GREAT COMMISSION
RESEARCH JOURNAL
2020, Vol. 12(1) 101-103

BOOK REVIEW

The Hospitable Leader: Creating Environments where People and Dreams Can Flourish.

By Smith, Terry A.
Bloomington, MN: Bethany House, 2018.
230pp.
US$17.99.

Reviewed by Harvey Mitchell Jr. who received his B.A. in Pastoral Ministries from Central Bible College in Springfield, MO., MDiv. from Fresno Pacific University in Fresno, CA., and is currently a DMin. student at Biola University. He has served in numerous positions at churches in California and Missouri including two lead pastor positions. He currently lives in Inner City St Louis with his wife Karissa.

Terry A. Smith has served as lead pastor of The Life Christian Church in the New York City metropolitan area for twenty-seven years. TLCC is a nondenominational faith community known for its vibrant diversity and robust leadership culture, with people from more than 132 distinct communities in the New York metro area participating in the life of the church. He holds a bachelor's degree in Organizational Management (Church Studies) and an MA in Organizational Leadership.

Smith says "Hospitable leaders view life and leadership through the lens of hospitality. They aspire to create environments of welcome where moral leadership can be exercised in all its permutations. These environments can be physical, even literal feasts perhaps, but even more they are spiritual, attitudinal, and communicative." (20) The author then lays out the outline for the book where he categorizes the 5 ways to extend hospitality: 1. Welcome Home, 2. Welcome Strangers, 3. Welcome Dreams, 4. Welcome Communication, and 5. Welcome Feasts (22, 23).

The author tells us hospitable leaders care not just about their dreams but also the dreams of those they lead. When a leader begins to realize that their success is directly connected to the success of those that follow them, the leader begins to take interest in the passion and dreams of those they lead. This adds to the leader's dreams and passion. For people to believe that the leader cares about them and their dreams, the leader must begin to welcome them home (to a place) and begin to warm their hearts like the warmth of home (45). Once someone feels at home, they will begin to follow at a higher level. The author suggests, "practicing leadership with a hospitality mindset is the right way—the moral way—to lead people. It is the community with purpose, fellowship with outcomes, hospitality with results." (39)

Part of helping people feel at home is learning to welcome the stranger. The author's working definition of a stranger is, "anyone who seems strange to you. Or to whom you may seem strange." (63) Only when people have been accepted and given a place and a seat at the table can we really learn and grow from our shared experiences and interactions.

We then begin to create an environment where people and dreams can flourish: "Hospitable leaders are hospitable to people and to their dreams. We love it when we find ourselves leading people whose heads and hearts are full of dreams." (94) Part of our calling as hospitable leaders is to help people discover their unique calling and giftings that will begin to help them understand "place" and ultimately discover the God given dreams that were inside of them. As leaders, our job is to call people out to great dreams and then greatly encourage them (126).

The last part is to learn how to enjoy all of life, the struggles as well as the blessings (202). In the last chapter, the author wraps up the idea of the hospitable leader welcoming people home in four things: 1) Be at peace with the fact that happiness is experienced in anticipation. 2) Anticipation opens us to the possibility. 3) Hope moves us to faith—

and when we have faith, possibility becomes reality. 4) Always hope for more (218).

The author's background is in leading a multiculturally diverse congregation where he has lived out the leadership lessons in this book. The only bias by the author was his excitement for his model of leadership that he calls "The Hospitable Leader," It felt like there was overlap between the servant leadership model and the author's model.

People should read Smith's book because even though his model sounds similar to the servant leader model, he does have some new and fresh ideas pertaining to leading diverse groups of people. The weakness of the book is that it could have been more concise. Some of the chapters felt redundant. However, the overall book was great. I would recommend this book to anyone interested in leadership.

GREAT COMMISSION
RESEARCH JOURNAL
2020, Vol. 12(1) 104-107

BOOK REVIEW

Donald A. McGavran: A Biography of the Twentieth Century's Premier Missiologist.

By Gary McIntosh
Boca Raton, FL: Church Leader Insights, 2015.
384pp.
Paperback edition $46.60, Kindle edition $19.95.

Reviewed by Keith R. Sellers, D. Min. candidate in Church Growth and Multiplication at The Talbot School of Theology, missionary with WorldVenture Mission.

Very few are as qualified as Gary McIntosh to write a biography about the twentieth century's premier missiologist. McIntosh who holds a Ph.D. in Intercultural Studies from Fuller Theological Seminary has been teaching at Talbot School of Theology, Biola University in La Mirada, CA since 1986. Born in Damoh, India in 1897 to missionary parents, Donald McGavran grew up to follow his parents' footsteps of missionary ministry. His books and teaching inspired a whole generation of missionaries and pastors across the world.

In chapter 1 and 2 McIntosh recounts the first departure of Donald and Mary McGavran from Indiana to India and then weaves in a detailed history of the spiritual legacy, which they inherited from their grandparents and parents. He then describes Donald's birth, childhood, and his parents' adventures in missionary service. Included is his education at Butler College and Yale University as well as his brief military experience at the close of World War I.

In chapter 3, *Serving as a Missionary,* McIntosh resumes the narrative from chapter 1 about Donald and Mary's departure to India where they set out to improve the education of Indian students. The chapter tells how the tragic loss of their daughter Mary Theodora just before a furlough served as a catalyst for deepening Donald's relationship with God and igniting his fervor for the lost (Kindle Loc. 1238-1248).

Chapter 4 recollects his continuing work among the *Satnamis* during the threat of WWII and severe economic depression. In chapter 5 the author describes McGavran's advancement to a professorship and how his research at Yale University led him to write, *Bridges of God,* which was dubbed the Magna Carta of the Church Growth Movement (Loc. 2033). As a pivotal chapter, it explains how McGavran's travels and research led him to pioneer the Institute of Church Growth at Northwest Christian College in Eugene, Oregon.

Chapters 6,7, and 8 recount the struggles of the Institute of Church Growth and its eventual transfer to the School of World Mission at Fuller Theological Seminary in Pasadena, CA. McIntosh lists the events leading to the formation of McGavran's team of heavy hitter missionary scholars-- Ralph Winter, Charles Kraft, C. Peter Wagner, and Arthur Glasser. Chapter 8 explains McGavran's reluctance to open his school to U.S. pastors, and how Win Arn and C. Peter Wagner became vital forces for introducing church growth to North America.

Chapters 9 and 10 tell about the expansion of church growth teaching and seminars from North America to other parts of the world as Wagner and Arn took church growth instruction to newer levels and foreign places, which George G. Hunter predicted ahead of time (Loc. 3929). Chapter 11, *Leaving a Legacy,* describes the prolific growth of the movement beyond Fuller's School of World Mission to denominational institutions and numerous outside publications. The book closes with Donald and Mary McGavran's home going in 1990 as well as seven important contributions of Donald McGavran's legacy that are still relevant today.

Pastors, educators, and missionaries who are looking for inspiration in ministry will find that the biography provides significant detail on a most inspirational figure. Those not well versed in missiology may miss the relevance of the names and places mentioned in chapters 8 and 9. Such readers should treat names like Winter, Glasser, Kraft, Hiebert, and Tippet as a suggested bibliography for future reading since they all became important contributors to the emerging field of missiology. Their missiological studies became the real foundation for the modern Church Growth Movement in North America. Some readers may accuse McIntosh of being biased toward McGavran and his teachings, but McIntosh does mention the most common criticisms (Ch.5, Loc. 2398-2443), and he even provides a list of publications, which attacked the Church Growth Movement in its early days (Ch.9, Loc. 4249-55). Some readers may find the lists of church growth publications in chapter 11 as a helpful archive, while other readers may want to skip over them. The book functions as an indirect and effective apologetic for the Church Growth Movement.

Pastors, theologians, educators, missionaries, and Christian workers of all specialties will glean many significant lessons from the book. As both a scholar and practitioner, McGavran attempted the profoundly neglected task of marrying theology with missions. Contrary to popular misconception, church growth instruction started as a technical discipline, which was rooted in biblical theology, not in the church marketing trends of the 1980s and 1990s. Nobody can accuse McGavran of having little concern for the downtrodden since much of his early ministry was focused on the education of the poor in India. As a child he witnessed his parents' care of suffering orphans as well as their devotion to rescuing their souls (Chapter 2). Critics cannot justifiably brand his homogenous unit principle as rooted in racism since it was presented as a way to reach more races, not push groups away (Ch.9, Loc. 4217-23). He reasoned that people are more likely to come to Christ when unnecessary social barriers are removed. His movements across denominational lines and his promotion of indigenous ministry demonstrate that he did not hold a triumphalist motivation (Ch.11, Loc. 5232). His influence reached both liberals and conservatives, and both wings criticized him (Ch.5, Loc. 2385-2416). As a man of his times, McGavran believed that scientific research could unlock the discovery of important principles of evangelism, however, his research orientation did not dilute his passion for prayer and dependence on the Holy Spirit. He even wrote devotionals and prayer guides for missionaries so that they might experience God's power in evangelism (Ch. 3, Loc. 1380-1411). His use of anthropology and sociology in evangelism fulfilled his purpose of reaching people.

As a worthy read, the book provides an incarnational apologetic for the causes of evangelism, assimilation of new believers, church planting and multiplication, and the pursuit of people movements throughout the world. This presentation of a life well lived is perhaps one of the best arguments for Christians to take up the cause of Christ and his Great Commission.

GREAT COMMISSION
RESEARCH JOURNAL
2020, Vol. 12(1) 108-110

BOOK REVIEW

Planting Reproducing Churches.

By Towns, Elmer L.
Shippensburg, PA: Destiny Image Publishers, 2018.
261pp.
US$16.99.

Reviewed by David Thiessen who serves as the executive pastor at Mountain View Church in Fresno, California. He is a doctor of ministry student in church growth at the Talbot School of Theology at Biola University.

Elmer Towns' thesis for the book is: "God still uses the average man, with limited resources, against insurmountable obstacles, in unlikely circumstances, to build a church for the glory of God" (105).

The book is divided into three sections. Part One, "The Foundation of Reproducing Churches," explores the foundations for church planting in Jesus' commitment to build His church and the five expressions of the Great Commission. Various methods of successful church planting from around the world are explored including planting independent churches, agency church planting, and media (online) church planting. Chapter three in particular is devoted to the miraculous growth of Yoido Full Gospel Church in Korea and its church planting efforts locally and globally. Chapter four focuses on the Great Commission, examining its five expressions in the Gospels and Acts in some detail and establishing it as the biblical mandate that must drive the establishment of new churches. This section concludes with general principles for church planting and the characteristics of church planters—those with evangelistic gifts, a clear call, and leadership capacity.

Part Two focuses on various types of church planting. Particular attention is given to the more recent trend of multisite church planting. Seacoast Church in South Carolina is identified as "the first example of a multisite church in the United States" (119), and its approach is surveyed. House church planting is also evaluated and the well-known success of this model in China is highlighted. Surprisingly, the third 'model' of church planting to be examined is the church split. All three types of church planting models are evaluated with lists of advantages and disadvantages.

Part Three, "Tools for Successful Church Planting," begins with the following definition of a church as "an assembly of professing followers of Jesus Christ; He lives in them, and they minister under the discipline of the Word of God. A church is organized to carry out the Great Commission by evangelism, teaching fellowship, worship, administering the ordinances, and reflecting the spiritual gift of ministry" (179). This definition is then unpacked in detail. The final chapter offers 46 practical steps for planting a church with a particular emphasis on choosing the right community to plant in, handling finances, and finding property for a permanent facility.

In terms of strengths, the author's discussion of the Great Commission in its five biblical expressions (John 20:19-21; Mark 16:14-16; Matthew 28:16-20; Luke 24:46-50; Acts 1:6-9) is a highlight of this book. The priority of this disciple-making mandate for church planting is made clear, and it is followed by an interesting discussion of what is not included in the Great Commission, highlighting the freedom of expression that church planters have. For instance, "The Great Commission tells us to teach all new converts, but it doesn't give us lesson plans or educational tools" (79).

Another strength of this book is the author's ability to ask excellent questions regarding the future reproductive capacity and sustainability of various church planting models in Part Two of the book. Regarding the multi-site model he asks, "What happens when the original pioneer dies or moves on? Will the second and third generations be able to carry on as effectively as the first generation?" (131). Imminently practical is the section on how to handle finances in the concluding chapter. Church planters are challenged to have a stewardship campaign in their first year, thereby teaching the whole church the importance of giving, commitment, and sacrifice right from the start (231).

The importance that the author places on house church planting is clear. It is highlighted throughout the book, and it is indisputably one of the major global church planting strategies being employed today. The unique contribution of house church planting is defended by highlighting its reproductive potential and its relevance across time and culture. As the author aptly states, "The house church is never out of style because a house was not conceived to be stylish. Also, the house church is never out of date because from the beginning people have needed a house to live in" (158). However, the author does not let his commitment to house church planting cloud his ability to evaluate its shortcomings. He includes a listing of seven weaknesses of house churches including a tendency towards lack of organization, doctrinal clarity, goals in ministry, and written standards for life and ministry (154-155).

What weakens the overall discussion of house church planting, unfortunately, is that the author's definition of what constitutes a true house church is unclear. Another difficulty arises when numerous statistics about house churches are cited without a source, "Approximately 93 percent of the members lead out in spoken prayer...90% will read from the Bible...87% will spend time sharing their personal needs and experiences" (144). These seem to be very specific percentages, and one assumes they were generated by a survey, but the source of the data remains a mystery. A last critique of the book is that the trends of culture are sometimes too easily accepted as requiring adaptation by the church for the sake of mission.

All in all, *Planting Reproducing Churches* provides a variety of helpful insights from an experienced observer of global church planting across multiple decades. A quick read, it will be helpful for those considering church planting as a part of their future ministry.

GREAT COMMISSION
RESEARCH JOURNAL
2020, Vol. 12(1) 111-113

BOOK REVIEW

The Return of Oral Hermeneutics: As Good Today as It Was for the Hebrew Bible and First-Century Christianity.

By Stephen, T.A., & Bjoraker, W.
Wipf & Stock, 2020

Reviewed by Regina Manley author of Bible StoryFire audio/video series. Regina lived overseas for 18 years serving with Mission Aviation Fellowship (MAF). She worked as MAF's orality consultant which included training through Bible story and discussion workshops for 12 years in 17 countries and the USA. She is now with Paraclete Mission Group, a doctoral candidate at Boise State University (Curriculum & Instruction), and holds degrees in Spanish (BA, La Verne University) and Applied Linguistics (MA, Biola University).

In *The Return of Oral Hermeneutics* Steffen and Bjoraker claim the oral approach is the best fit for studying Scripture because of its ability to maximize communication and impact. They consider it a "crucial complementor" (p. 304) to traditional, or what they term, "textual hermeneutics" which relies on propositional-based textual analysis, grammar and word studies, and systematic theology (pp. 14-18).

Steffen worked among the newly literate Ifugao in the Philippines. Influenced by Trevor McIlwain, he replaced propositional teaching and outlines for a story-centric model. Bjoraker's ministry was to highly educated Jews. At first, he considered using stories as irrelevant.

He now recognizes biblical narratives and discussion as "the best approach I have ever discovered for engaging Jewish seekers with the Word of God" (p. xxii). The wide applicability of oral hermeneutics (OH) makes this book a must-read for anyone working cross-culturally, across generations, or training others for ministry.

The book is divided into three parts. In the first and last parts the authors present an experiential dive into two Bible stories. Bjoraker demonstrates OH in action with a group of professionals. These transcribed sessions are each followed by reflections. The reflections in Part One highlight how OH engages the whole brain by activating the emotional, relational, imaginative, experiential, visual and sensory areas through narrative and dialog.

Part two, the largest portion, elucidates the propositions supporting this radical shift. First, the authors challenge common biases formed through school culture by introducing us to the world of orality that influenced the formation of the Old and New Testament texts. They document oral-communal-liturgical processes customary to instruction through the centuries prior to the printing press.

Next, they describe the parameters of OH. Narrative is capable of embodying meaning in ways people can identify with, be challenged by, and remember. It can be powerfully enhanced by artistic expression. The metanarrative of Scripture acts as a boundary, with the whole informing the parts and the parts informing the whole. Then they explain how making narrative central and prioritizing participants' insights leads to an alternate way of theologizing.

Traditional hermeneutics analyzes and systematizes, culminating in abstract principles such as God is love. In comparison, OH invites listeners to identify with and discuss the stories of God interacting with people. Character theology recognizes that anyone who can understand a Bible story can discover the truths it entails. This middle section ends by focusing on questions including how to form character-centric questions that encourage "relational-building dialogue" and lead to "application, memory, and reproducibility" (p. 207). In fact, questions feature prominently in the entire book.

The Return of Oral Hermeneutics is an entertaining read. The writing will appeal to the lay reader but also contains extensive footnotes for the more serious exegete. This book is feasible as a seminary or Bible school textbook.

Readers would have benefitted by including more examples of varieties of OH currently practiced which the authors alluded to in chapter four. In addition, there is much to be explored about facilitating discovery learning. How does one manage the unpredictable dynamics that can occur in group dialog? Assess progress? Cover aspects missed by the group?

Adopting an OH will be difficult for those accustomed to a central role as lecturer or teacher. It will be an easier fit for those who mentor and are keen listeners, skilled at "reading" and interacting with people.

The orality movement has gained many advocates in Christian work and mission over the last decades, but Steffen and Bjoraker have produced the most comprehensive apologetic I have seen to date. They both demonstrate OH and describe the principles behind why it is a robust, viable tool. Going far beyond those who cannot, do not or will not learn from reading, they explain why OH is effective for widely diverse audiences including highly-educated professionals, digitally-preferenced moderns, and post-millennials. As a reader, *be prepared for a paradigm shift*; some of those stones Steffen and Bjoraker upturn, may be supporting your foundation.

GREAT COMMISSION RESEARCH NETWORK
(formerly: The American Society for Church Growth)

OFFICERS

President:
Dr. Jay Moon
Professor of Church Planting and Evangelism
Asbury Theological Seminary
Email: jay.moon@asburyseminary.edu

First Vice President:
Dr. Winfield Bevins
Director, Asbury Seminary Church Planting Initiative
Email: winfield.bevins@asburyseminary.edu

Second Vice President:
Dr. Brad Ransom
Chief Training Officer
Director of Church Planting
Free Will Baptist North American Ministries
Email: brad@nafwb.org

Treasurer:
Ben Penfold
Chief Executive Officer
Penfold & Company

GREAT COMMISSION RESEARCH NETWORK

greatcommissionresearch.com

MEMBERSHIP

What is the Great Commission Research Network?

The Great Commission Research Network (GCRN) is a worldwide and professional association of Christian leaders whose ministry activities have been influenced by the basic and key principles of church growth as originally developed by the late Donald McGavran. Founded by renowned missiologists George G. Hunter III and C. Peter Wagner, the GCRN has expanded into an affiliation of church leaders who share research, examine case studies, dialogue with cutting-edge leaders, and network with fellow church professionals who are committed to helping local churches expand the kingdom through disciple-making.

Who Can Join the GCRN?

GCRN membership is open to all who wish a professional affiliation with colleagues in the field. The membership includes theoreticians, such as professors of evangelism and missions, and practitioners, such as pastors, denominational executives, parachurch leaders, church planters, researchers, mission leaders, and consultants. Some members specialize in domestic or mono-cultural church growth, while others are cross-culturally oriented.

Why Join the GCRN?

The GCRN provides a forum for maximum interaction among leaders, ministries, and resources on the cutting edge of Great Commission research. The annual conference of the GCRN (typically held in March each year) offers the opportunity for research updates and information on new resources and developments, as well as fellowship and encouragement from colleagues in the field of church growth. Membership in the GCRN includes a subscription to the *Great*

Commission Research Journal and a discount for the annual conference.

How Do I Join the GCRN?

For further information on membership and the annual conference, please visit greatcommissionresearch.com.

Membership Fees

- One-year regular membership (inside or outside USA) - $59
- One-year student/senior adult membership (inside or outside USA) - $39
- Three-year regular membership (inside or outside USA) - $177
- Three-year senior membership (inside or outside USA) - $117
- Membership includes a subscription to the *Great Commission Research Journal* which is in the process of transitioning to an electronic format.

GREAT COMMISSION RESEARCH NETWORK

AWARDS

Donald A. McGavran Award for Outstanding Leadership in Great Commission Research

Normally once each year, the GCRN gives this award to an individual for exemplary scholarship, intellect, and leadership in the research and dissemination of the principles of effective disciple-making as described by Donald A. McGavran. The award recipients to date:

Win Arn	1989	Rick Warren	2004
C. Peter Wagner	1990	Charles Arn	2005
Carl F. George	1991	John Vaughan	2006
Wilbert S. McKinley	1992	Waldo Werning	2006
Robert Logan	1993	Bob Whitesel	2007
Bill Sullivan	1994	Bill Easum	2009
Elmer Towns	1994	Thom S. Rainer	2010
Flavil R. Yeakley Jr.	1995	Ed Stetzer	2012
George G. Hunter III	1996	Nelson Searcy	2013
Eddie Gibbs	1997	J. D. Payne	2014
Gary L. McIntosh	1998	Alan McMahan	2015
Kent R. Hunter	1999	Steve Wilkes	2016
R. Daniel Reeves	2000	Art McPhee	2016
Ray Ellis	2002	Mike Morris	2017
John Ellas	2003	Bill Day	2019

Win Arn Lifetime Achievement Award in Great Commission Research

This award is given to a person who has excelled in the field of American church growth over a long period of time. The award recipients to date:

Eddie Gibbs	2011	Gary McIntosh	2015
Elmer Towns	2012	Kent R. Hunter	2017
George G. Hunter III	2013	Carl George	2019
John Vaughan	2014		

American Society for Church Growth/GCRN Past Presidents

C. Peter Wagner	1986	Ray W. Ellis	1999-00
George G. Hunter III	1987	Charles Van Engen	2001-02
Kent R. Hunter	1988	Charles Arn	2003-04
Elmer Towns	1989	Alan McMahan	2005-06
Eddie Gibbs	1990	Eric Baumgartner	2007-08
Bill Sullivan	1991	Bob Whitesel	2009-12
Carl F. George	1992	Steve Wilkes	2013-14
Flavil Yeakley Jr.	1993	Mike Morris	2015-16
John Vaughan	1994	James Cho	2017-18
Gary L. McIntosh	1995-96	Gordon Penfold	2019-20
R. Daniel Reeves	1997-98		

GREAT COMMISSION RESEARCH NETWORK

SUBMISSIONS

The *Great Commission Research Journal* publishes both peer-reviewed articles reporting original research and reviews of recent books relevant to evangelism and disciple making.

The scope of the journal includes research focusing on evangelism, church planting, church growth, spiritual formation, church renewal, worship, or missions. Articles come from both members and non-members of the Great Commission Research Network and are generally unsolicited submissions, which are welcomed and will be considered for peer-review. There is no charge for submission or publication.

ARTICLES

All submissions should be emailed to the editor, David R. Dunaetz at ddunaetz@apu.edu.

Peer Review Process

Only the highest quality submissions presenting original research within the scope of the journal will be chosen for publication. To ensure this, all articles will go through a peer review process. Articles deemed by the editor to have potential for publication will be sent to reviewers (members of the editorial board or other reviewers with the needed expertise) for their recommendation. Upon receiving the reviewers' recommendations, the author will be notified that the submission was either rejected, that the submission has potential but needs to be significantly revised and resubmitted, that the submission is conditionally accepted if the noted issues are addressed, or that the submission is accepted unconditionally.

Format

Papers should be APA formatted according to the 7th edition of the Publication Manual of the American Psychological Association. Submissions should include a cover page, be double-spaced in Times New Roman, and be between 3,000 and 7,000 words (approximately 10-22 pages) in .docx format. Contact the editor for exceptions to this word count.

In-text references should be in the form (Smith, 2020) or (Smith, 2020, p.100). At the end of the article should be a References section. No footnotes should be used. Minimize the use of endnotes. If endnotes are necessary, more than two or three are strongly discouraged; rather than using Microsoft Word's endnote tool, place them manually before the References section.

Include an abstract of approximately 100-150 words at the beginning of your text.

After the References section, include a short biography (approximately 30 words) for each author.

BOOK REVIEWS

The purpose of our book reviews is to direct the reader to books that contribute to the broader disciple making endeavors of the church. The review (500-2000 words) is to help potential readers understand how the book will contribute to their ministry, especially those in North America or which have a large cross-cultural base. The review should consist of a summary of the contents, an evaluation of the book, and a description of how the book is applicable to practitioners. Before submitting a book review, please contact the book review editor Dr. Kelton Hinton (khinton247@gmail.com) to either propose a book to be reviewed or to ask if there is a book that needs to be reviewed.

COPYRIGHT

Copyrights on articles are held by the Great Commission Research Network with permission to republish given to the authors. Requests for permission to reproduce material from the journal, except for brief quotations in scholarly reviews and publications, should be directed to the general editor of the journal.

CONTACT INFORMATION

To submit an article or for general questions, contact:
Dr. David Dunaetz, ddunaetz@apu.edu

For questions about book reviews, contact:
Dr. Kelton Hinton, khinton247@gmail.com

Made in the USA
Monee, IL
03 November 2020

46663725R00069